$SOS + R$

The **S**wallow, the **O**wl, the **S**andpiper
...and the Little Red **R**obin

sandpiper

The Swallow, the Owl, the Sandpiper and the Little Red Robin   ISBN 978-1-7393594-2-3
Published by Finks Publishing. Distributed by Sandpiper.
Illustrated by Derek Robertson
First edition published 2023
Scottish Charity no. SCO 31165
© Sandpiper
www.sandpipertrust.org

Praise for *The Swallow, the Owl and the Sandpiper* **- Volume One**

'Buy this book, you won't regret it.'

'I bought one of these remarkable books and wanted another dozen to give to some of my friends, it is a book that should be in every household for adults, teenagers and younger children to pick up and dip into. Full of thought provoking poems, and prose that will make you laugh and cry - this book has soul.'

'I keep it at the side of my bed- and its something to dip into when I'm having a bad night. It's such a gentle book.'

'This book is a gem, I simply couldn't put it down. I read it cover to cover in a day. It now sits on my table where I can pick it up and read again and again - for inspiration or to just get past a bad moment in my day. I thoroughly recommend it, buy it now, you'll not be disappointed.'

'Great bedside read! There are so many lovely poems and sayings which fit your every mood. I highly recommend it as a book to dip into.'

'This is a fantastic collection of poetry, words of wisdom and encouragement for people from all walks of life. I throughly recommend this book and one to be kept close at all times.'

*Dedicated to the world of pre-hospital care in Scotland
and to those who strive on a daily basis to save the lives of others.*

Foreword

Late in the afternoon of Sunday 11th September 2022 I found myself standing outside the front door of the Palace of Holyroodhouse, waiting for the arrival of the hearse carrying the coffin of Her late Majesty The Queen. It was a moment that had been long in the planning, but the television cameras mounted on hastily constructed platforms around the forecourt and the sheer volume of people cramming either side of the Royal Mile beyond the gates confirmed that this was no rehearsal. As did the tension and emotion unexpectedly etched into the faces of waiting soldiers and staff alike. I realised at that point that one of my roles would be to keep calm and to offer reassurance to those around me. I've stood at many a church or crematorium door over the years, waiting for the hearse, and supported many a circle of family and friends in their sadness and sorrow. This was different, and yet not so very different.

I can't help hoping that this book in its own way might prove a source of calm and reassurance in the face of tension and emotion, at a time of sadness and sorrow. Not least in its capacity to transport the reader to calm and reassuring places. One of the most powerful consequences of Queen Elizabeth's peaceful death at Balmoral was the long and poignant journey by road to Edinburgh, passing through or by some of Scotland's most vivid landscapes on the way. From the hills and glens of the Highlands to the rolling fields and riverbanks of the lowlands, all basked for once in glorious sunshine, there was a prevailing sense of nature and the cycle of the seasons supplying their own timeless means of comfort and strength.

Death rarely comes quite so peacefully, and no matter how well-rehearsed and ready we think of ourselves for the moment of letting go, it can still prompt unexpected levels of tension and emotion. The words - and the pictures they paint – contained within these pages can surely be another timeless means of comfort and strength, of calm and reassurance, and I commend them warmly and gratefully.

The Revd Neil N Gardner DL MA BD
Minister of Canongate Kirk, the Kirk of Holyroodhouse and Edinburgh Castle
Domestic Chaplain to HM The King in Scotland

Introduction

On 18th December 2014, my husband Robin, underwent spinal surgery to remove a small benign tumour from the lower back.

We had no qualms about the operation. Prior to his surgery Robin was told he would be back driving two weeks later

The operation was due to be completed by 4pm, so my younger son, Jack, and I spent 5 hours waiting for news about him. We spent this time sitting in the newly completed Sandpiper Sanctuary, yet to be open to the public. The sanctuary houses the most beautiful, colourful, thought provoking stained glass window featuring a 'fish eye' view of the landscape, within the extensive catchment area of Aberdeen Royal Infirmary stretching from the Cairngorms in the west, up to the Northern Isles, the East down the spectacular coast the farmland of the Mearns in the South. This specially designed room, adjacent to the Emergency department, provides a much needed contemplative space away from the hustle and bustle of the hospital. How strange was it therefore that the Maitland family were the first family to make use of it.

The call we had spent 8 hours waiting for finally came through from the neurosurgeon.

"The operation was successful but it appears there are some complications" to this day those words continue to reverberate around my mind.

My younger son walked quickly up to the ward keen to see his father and to hear more news, whilst strangely enough my footsteps dragged, dreading the reality of the words we were about to hear. Absolutely nothing, could have prepared me for the news that we were about to be given.

After listening to the shock of the words delivered to us by the surgeon, we were allowed in to see my husband. In his own words, Robin exclaimed, "Meet the new Professor Stephen Hawkins. I may not have his brain but I certainly have his body." A shocking introduction to the life of a quadriplegic. The following morning we were woken early by a phone call from the hospital asking us to get there quickly as Robin was panicking and asking for a knife. He was terrified and wanted out. He felt he was tied to the bed and wanted us to cut him free.

Close family were called as Robin's condition continued to deteriorate.

It was clear he was going into respiratory failure. The decision was taken to place him on a ventilator in an induced coma in order to transfer him to a specialist spinal unit in Glasgow. We said our goodbyes as the consultant warned us that there could be further complications if and when he woke from his coma.

This was Christmas Eve 2014. Celebratory decorations wherever we looked. Joy, laughter and present swapping amongst the staff. On arrival we discovered that the consultant was just leaving to go out for a Christmas dinner. She was stopped to speak to us. We were told that on first glance at his scans, Robin had suffered a neck injury similar to someone who had been in a motorbike accident. We, of course, knew otherwise.

He remained on a ventilator for 2 weeks. Very slowly he was woken from his deep sleep. The first couple of days were terrifying as it was thought he had suffered some brain damage and therefore struggled to communicate with us. Very slowly his speech returned, but he still remained very poorly. Robin was adamant that he could survive without being able to move his body, but not his brain, so it was a huge relief to us that slowly his brain returned to normal, along with his wonderful wit.

Days turned into weeks, weeks into months, and months in to 5 years, 2 ½ of those spent in different hospitals.

At last after no less than 862 nights hospitalised, he was discharged home where he was welcomed by his family and his wonderful team of carers who looked after him around the clock. They were the only reason that Robin's health stabilised and he spent a year at home with no hospital visits.

At the beginning I had hope in my heart that Robin's condition would improve, that he would regain strength to move, but as time passed so did my hope as quite literally it melted away. To this day I flinch every time I hear the word "HOPE". To keep hope in one's heart can so often lead to feelings of disappointment, and believe me, there were many of those. I did however keep faith in my heart throughout. We were surrounded by so much kindness both from strangers and from the nursing staff in the hospitals.

Robin was never given any specific diagnosis. Not even by searching every alleyway for answers. At first it was thought he had suffered trauma to the neck, and then it was thought he had a sudden rare auto immune disease. To this day we have no understanding of what happened whilst Robin was in surgery. Every day I watched him suffer excruciating pain. Some days were better than others and we grabbed the good days with hungry hearts. We crowdfunded in order to allow him to sit up front in an especially converted van, all thanks to the generosity of good friends. We were able to take him for drives. Just looking out over the changing crops throughout the seasons was enough to satisfy Robin's boredom. Our biggest adventures were made to our son's wedding in Edinburgh and also to see Scotland winning the Calcutta Cup at Murrayfield.

Robin's love of rugby brought our Sandpiper Patron, Gavin Hastings into our lives and for this deepening friendship I will always be grateful.

So, how did I cope...

Words that come to mind.

Disbelief, shock, desperation, despair mixed up with the overpowering feelings of determination to move mountains to heal Robin.

Feelings of exhaustion were also overpowering and came in waves. Sleep, sleep, sleep has always been my form of escapism. But, then I would wake from this nightmare. There was no nightmare. Reality needed to be faced.

When awake I poured all my energy into finding a cure for Robin. My determination to do this knew no bounds. As you know when the worst happens, the world keeps spinning, but for us, it was like we were stuck in a quagmire of slurry, unable to turn right or left.

Hogmanay 2014: he was in Intensive Care in his most critical state. As a family we were allowed to see him - albeit briefly. It was not in our nature to do so, but we placed our hands on him, holding one another and we silently sent him healing messages of strength. We were also aware that many friends were raising their glasses to him as Big Ben struck midnight. Coincidence or not, in the morning he was stronger and it was then that they very slowly woke him from his coma. A week later he uttered his first words to us. Despite being told that the swelling in his neck might have affected his brain and his ability to speak, he was back with us.

My waking day was spent either with him or researching worldwide how to find a cure for him. England, America, Switzerland, Germany; I spoke to experts in the field of neurology to try and find answers… but I failed. No-one, but no-one could shed light on what had happened to Robin. Down every explored avenue I was met by a dead end.

I sought solace amongst family and friends who knew and loved Robin. This included many Sandpiper doctors who had become friends since *Sandpiper* was founded. Doctors, paramedics and nurses living and working in our rural Scottish communities, or in the Emergency Department in Aberdeen. No answers, but massive support was gifted by all.

More often than not I craved to be on my own. I would frequently stop in laybys on my way home where I would shed more tears than I knew I had stored in my tear tank. I cried, I screamed….yet, I was never angry.

During the 100s of hours I spent at Robin's hospital bedside, I was often asked to sit in the waiting room whilst Robin underwent procedures. In order to focus my mind, I would search for different phrases, poetry and words of wisdom that I could gain strength and understanding from. God Bless all who wrote them, because they have been my saviour. Little did I know then that this was a very early start to compiling a second book following on from *The Swallow, The Owl and The Sandpiper*. It was a few years later that I decided to add *The Little Red Robin* to the title.

This collection of words has been an integral part of my journey through grief and bereavement.

Robin passed away in August 2019. We were all with him holding his hands when he reluctantly left us.

The painstaking journey through grief and bereavement is, quite literally, tortuous, but it is one we all have to travel through at some stage in our lives.

In the beginning I could not work out who I was grieving for. Could it be possible that I was grieving for one person twice over? For the healthy, loving, witty Robin prior to his operation or for the Robin who had suffered catastrophic injuries under anaesthetic rendering him paraplegic for the last 5 years of his precious life. In times of trouble I have slowly learned to live in the moment, to take one day at a time. There is no way to avoid the pain of this journey. The world keeps spinning and somehow we have to learn to spin with it.

I find comfort in my home, our home which we shared for 30 years, surrounded by my beloved four legged friends. I watch the seasons as they come and go, I listen to the birds who give me enormous pleasure, but most of all I watch my children, Robin's children. Through them, I live with him and I see him in each and every one of them. The way they walk, the way they talk. They share his humour, his interests and also his compassion. And yes, I can even see him in his grandchildren.

When I compiled my first book, *The Swallow, The Owl and The Sandpiper* it was my hope that it would bring comfort to anyone with sadness in their hearts. I have been overwhelmed by the messages from those who enjoyed it. The words inside this new book will bring comfort and perhaps a smile to those who delve into it.

All proceeds from sales of the book will yet again go to *Sandpiper*.

Claire Maitland MBE – Sandpiper

A message from our Patron

As patron of *Sandpiper* since 2001, I am honoured to introduce this second book compiled by Claire Maitland. The first book, *The Swallow, The Owl and The Sandpiper* has travelled far and wide reaching every corner of the globe.

Sorrow is sadly part of life, and is a feeling that we will all endure at some stage. There are appropriate heart felt words for everyone is this first book.

This second compilation of words, titled *The Swallow, The Owl, The Sandpiper and The Little Red Robin*, will, without fail provide those who are experiencing sadness, confusion or worry with equally felt words of courage, wisdom, spirit together with the resilience of The Little Red Robin.

The funds raised by the sales of this book will again enable Sandpiper to continue to support our clinical responders by providing them with the necessary equipment to save to help lives.

Every day across Scotland our responders are being called to 999 medical emergencies so hundreds of patients benefit each year.

Our responders save lives and enhance outcomes by reaching the patient quickly, with the right clinical skills and equipment to perform swift immediate interventions, therefore stabilising the patient prior to transfer to hospital.

I hope this book spreads its wings to provide a little comfort for those in need, be it from the words on these pages or the emergency care that this charity provides.

Gavin Hastings OBE – *Sandpiper Patron*

...love from Annie

While the global health pandemic over the last few years has tested our capacity for endurance, perhaps it is in these times of crisis that we find ourselves compelled to challenge our individual and collective fragilities and strengths more than ever. In doing so, we might discover potential solutions to manage deep uncertainty.

When things we can sometimes take for granted – our health, security and sustainability, our relationships with family and friends and our veritable existence – are being tested, is it still possible to find comfort and a lasting sense of stability and peace?

Our connection to one another can ease and comfort us, especially when everything else seems to be falling apart.

Yet, ultimately, we have to dig deep within ourselves in order to access The Swallow of courage, The Owl of wisdom, The Sandpiper of spirit, and finally The Little Red Robin of resilience.

These qualities are the alchemic entities we can all call upon in order to survive through the most difficult circumstances.

Claire Maitland knows a great deal about this. She has been called to draw from them in ways that she least would have expected. It is from a deep well of human experience that she has been able to transform overwhelming circumstances. Claire's latest book is testimony to her strength, courage, fortitude and love.

May you find it as inspirational and restorative as I do...

Love Annie Lennox OBE - *Singer songwriter*

The Swallow

courage

☙

Be like the bird, who
Pausing in her flight
Awhile on boughs too slight
Feels them give way beneath her,
And yet sings, knowing she hath wings
Victor Hugo

Make the Ordinary Come Alive *William Martin*

Do not ask your children
to strive for extraordinary lives.
Such striving may seem admirable,
but it is the way of foolishness.
Help them instead to find the wonder
and the marvel of an ordinary life.
Show them the joy of tasting
tomatoes, apples and pears.
Show them how to cry
when pets and people die.
Show them the infinite pleasure
in the touch of a hand.
And make the ordinary come alive for them.
The extraordinary will take care of itself.

cz

BE BRAVE ENOUGH TO START
A CONVERSATION THAT MATTERS *Margaret Wheatley*

cz

Give us grace and strength to forbear and to persevere
Robert Louis Stevenson

**"Give us grace and strength to forbear and to persevere.
Give us courage and gaiety, and the quiet mind. Spare to
us our friends, soften to our enemies. Bless us, if it may
be, in all our innocent endeavours. If it may not, give us
the strength to encounter that which is to come, that we
may be brave in peril, constant in tribulation, temperate
in wrath, and in all changes of fortune, and down to the
gates of death, loyal and loving to one another."**

Midwives of the Soul *Elena Mikhalkova*

My grandmother once gave me a tip:
In difficult times, you move forward in small steps.
Do what you have to do, but little by little.
Don't think about the future, or what may happen tomorrow.
Wash the dishes.
Remove the dust.
Write a letter.
Make a soup.
You see?
You are advancing step by step.
Take a step and stop.
Rest a little.
Praise yourself.
Take another step.
Then another.
You won't notice, but your steps will grow more and more.
And the time will come when you can think about the future
without crying.

༼ༀ

Well, everyone can master
a grief but he that has it

William Shakespeare, **Much Ado About Nothing**

The Swallow

It has been said, 'time heals all wounds.'
I do not agree.
The wounds remain.
In time, the mind, protecting its sanity,
covers them with scar tissue
and the pain lessens.
But it is never gone

Rose Fitzgerald Kennedy

℘

Into the freedom of wind and sunshine
Ruth Burgess

Into the freedom of wind and sunshine
we let you go.
Into the dance of the stars and planets
we let you go.
Into the wind's breath and the hands of the star maker
we let you go.

We love you, we miss you, we want you to be happy;
go safely, go dancing, go running home.

Deep peace of the running wave **to you.**
Deep peace of the flowing air **to you.**
Deep peace of the quiet earth **to you.**
Deep peace of the Son of Peace **to you.**

As I sit in heaven *Hazel Birdsall*

And watch you everyday
I try to let you know with signs
I never went away
I hear you when you're laughing
And watch you as you sleep
I even place my arms around you
To calm you as you weep
I see you wish the days away
Begging to have me home
So I try to send you signs
So you know you're not alone
Don't feel guilty that you have
Life that was denied to me
Heaven is truly beautiful
Just you wait and see
So live your life, laugh again
Enjoy yourself, be free
Then I know with every breath you take
You'll be taking one for me.

༄

EN.DUR.ANCE (NOUN)
THE POWER TO WITHSTAND PAIN OR HARDSHIPS; THE ABILITY OR STRENGTH TO CONTINUE DESPITE PERSONAL FATIGUE, STRESS, AND OTHER ADVERSE CONDITIONS.

The Swallow

Your Spirit – a Tribute to My Father
Tram-Tiara T. Von Reichenbach

I know that no matter what
You will always be with me.
When life separates us
I'll know it is only your soul
Saying goodbye to your body
But your spirit will be with me always.
When I see a bird chirping on a nearby branch
I will know it is you singing to me.
When a butterfly brushes gently by me so care freely
I will know it is you assuring me you are free from pain.
When the gentle fragrance of a flower catches my attention
I will know it is you reminding me
To appreciate the simple things in life.
When the sun shining through my window awakens me
I will feel the warmth of your love.
When I hear the rain pitter patter against my window sill
I will hear your words of wisdom
And will remember what you taught me so well
That without rain trees cannot grow
Without rain flowers cannot bloom
Without life's challenges I cannot grow strong.
When I look out to the sea
I will think of your endless love for your family.
When I think of mountains, their majesty and magnificence
I will think of your courage for your country.
No matter where I am
Your spirit will be beside me
For I know that no matter what
You will always be with me.

೫

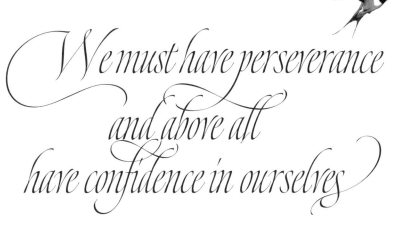

We must have perseverance and above all have confidence in ourselves

We must believe that we are gifted for something.

Marie Curie

∽

" My heart is so small
it's almost invisible.
How can You place
such big sorrows in it?"
" Look," He answered,
" your eyes are even smaller,
yet they behold the world."

Rumi

The Last Battle
Anon

If it should be that I grow frail and weak
And pain should keep me from my sleep,
Then will you do what must be done,
For this – the last battle – can't be won.
You will be sad I understand
But don't let grief stay your hand,
For on this day, more than the rest,
Your love and friendship must stand the test.
We have had so many happy years,
You wouldn't want me to suffer so.
When the time comes, please, let me go.

Take me to where my needs they'll tend,
Only, stay with me till the end
And hold me firm and speak to me
Until my eyes no longer see.
I know in time you will agree
It is a kindness you do to me.
Although my tail it's last has waved,
From pain and suffering I have been saved.
Don't grieve that it must be you
Who has to decide this thing to do;
We've been so close – we two – these years,
Don't let your heart hold any tears

❃

Giving up is easy.
It's trying even harder that's difficult

NOT EVERYTHING THAT IS FACED CAN BE CHANGED, BUT NOTHING CAN BE CHANGED UNTIL IT IS FACED.

James Baldwin

ଔ

For Equilibrium, a Blessing: *John O'Donohue,*
To Bless the Space Between Us: A Book of Blessings

Like the joy of the sea coming home to shore,
May the relief of laughter rinse through your soul.

As the wind loves to call things to dance,
May your gravity by lightened by grace.

Like the dignity of moonlight restoring the earth,
May your thoughts incline with reverence and respect.

As water takes whatever shape it is in,
So free may you be about who you become.

As silence smiles on the other side of what's said,
May your sense of irony bring perspective.

As time remains free of all that it frames,
May your mind stay clear of all it names.

May your prayer of listening deepen enough
to hear in the depths the laughter of god.

The Mountain *Laura Ding-Edwards*

If the mountain seems too big today
then climb a hill instead
if the morning brings you sadness
it's ok to stay in bed

> If the day ahead weighs heavy
> and your plans feel like a curse
> there's no shame in rearranging
> don't make yourself feel worse

If a shower stings like needles
and a bath feels like you'll drown
if you haven't washed your hair for days
don't throw away your crown

> A day is not a lifetime
> a rest is not defeat
> don't think of it as failure
> just a quiet, kind retreat

It's ok to take a moment
from an anxious, fractured mind
the world will not stop turning
while you get realigned

> The mountain will still be there
> when you want to try again
> you can climb it in your own time
> just love yourself til then

I Stood by your Bed Last Night
Anon

I stood by your bed last night;
I came to have a peep.
I could see that you were crying, you found it hard to sleep.
I spoke to you so softly as you brushed away a tear,
'It's me, I haven't left you, I'm well, I'm fine, I'm here.'

I was close to you at breakfast,
I watched you pour the tea.
You were thinking of the many times, your hands reached down to me.
I was with you at the shops today; your arms were getting sore.
I longed to take your parcels, I wish I could do more.
I was with you at my grave today; you tend it with such care.
I want to re-assure you, that I'm not lying there.

I flew with you towards our house, as you fumbled for your key.
I gently landed next to you; I smiled and said, 'it's me.'
You looked so very tired, and sank into a chair.
I tried so hard to let you know, that I was right there.

It's possible for me to be so near you everyday.
To say to you with certainty, 'I never went away.'
You sat there very quietly, then smiled, I think you knew…
in the stillness of that evening, I was very close to you.

The day is over…
I smile and watch you yawning and say 'good-night, God bless,
I'll see you in the morning.'
And when the time is right for you to cross the brief divide,
I'll fly across to greet you and we'll stand, side by side.
I have so many things to show you,
there is so much for you to see.
Be patient, live your journey out…
then come home to be with me

She Couldn't Feel her Wings *Atticus*

She couldn't feel her wings
but knew they were there
so she built a ladder
that led to the sky
and when she touched the clouds
she remembered how to fly.

☙

Some Days *Anon*

They tell me life's a journey
That will take me many years
Some days are filled with laughter
And some days are filled with tears

Some days I think my heart will break
That I can't persevere
Some days I have to don a mask
And hide beneath its veneer

Some days I turn and look for you
With thoughts I'd like to share
Some days I just can't understand
The reason you're not there

Some days the sadness leaves me
And my smile will reappear
Some days I close my eyes because
Your memory is so clear

Some days I struggle to go on
Just wishing you were near
Most days I spend in gratitude
That you were ever here.

Being a Nurse Means
Melodie Chenevert, RN

You will never be bored.
You will always be frustrated.
You will be surrounded by challenges.
So much to do and so little time.
You will carry immense responsibility
and very little authority.
You will step into people's lives
and you will make a difference.
Some will bless you.
Some will curse you.
You will see people at their worst –
and at their best.
You will never cease to be amazed
at people's capacity for
love, courage, and endurance.
You will see life begin – and end.
You will experience resounding triumphs
and devastating failures.
You will cry a lot.
You will laugh a lot.
You will know what it is to be human
and to be humane.

cx

THE OAK FOUGHT THE WIND AND WAS BROKEN, THE WILLOW BENT WHEN IT MUST AND SURVIVED

Robert Jordan

The True Meaning Of Life *Pat A. Fleming*

The Years have passed by,
In the blink of an eye,
Moments of sadness,
And joy have flown by.

People I loved,
Have come and have gone,
But the world never stopped,
And we all carried on.

Life wasn't easy,
And the struggles were there,
Filled with times that it mattered,
Times I just didn't care.

I stood on my own,
And I still found my way,
Through some nights filled with tears,
And the dawn of new days.

And now with old age,
It's become very clear,
Things I once found important,
Were not why I was here.

And how many things,
That I managed to buy,
Were never what made me,
Feel better inside.

And the worries and fears,
That plagued me each day,
In the end of it all,
Would just fade away.

But how much I reached out,
To others when needed,
Would be the true measure,
Of how I succeeded.

And how much I shared,
Of my soul and my heart,
Would ultimately be,
What set me apart.

And what's really important,
Is my opinion of me,
And whether or not,
I'm the best I can be.

And how much more kindness,
And love I can show,
Before the Lord tells me,
It's my time to go.

ભ

*When you are sorrowful
look again in your heart, and you shall see
that in truth you are weeping
for that which has been your delight.*

The Swallow

Being deeply loved by someone gives you strength, while loving someone deeply gives you courage *Lao Tzu*

☙

No one ever told me... *C.S. Lewis – A grief observed*

No one ever told me that grief felt so like fear. I am not afraid, but the sensation is like being afraid. The same fluttering in the stomach, the same restlessness, the yawning. I keep on swallowing. At other times it feels like being mildly drunk, or concussed. There is a sort of invisible blanket between the world and me. I find it hard to take in what anyone says. Or perhaps, hard to want to take it in. It is so uninteresting.

☙

There is something stronger than death, it's the presence of the memory of the living

Little Snowdrop *Anon*

The world may never notice
If a Snowdrop doesn't
bloom, Or even pause to
wonder If the petals fall too
soon.

But every life that ever
forms, Or ever comes to be,
Touches the world in some
small way For all eternity.

The little one we longed for
Was swiftly here and gone.
But the love that was then
planted Is a light that still
shines on.

And though our arms are
empty, Our hearts know
what to do. For every
beating of our hearts Says
that we love you.

℘

Someone told me... *Jennifer Worth*

"Someone once said that youth is wasted on the young. Not a bit of
it. Only the young have the impulsive energy to tackle the impossible
and enjoy it; the courage to follow their instincts and brave the new; the
stamina to work all day, all night and all the next day without tiring. For
the young everything is possible. None of us, twenty years later, could do
the things we did in our youth. Though the vision burns still bright, the
energy has gone."

Life's Tug Of War *Anon*

LIFE can seem ungrateful and not always kind.
LIFE can pull at your heartstrings and play with your mind.
LIFE can be blissful and happy and free.
LIFE can put beauty in the things that you see.
LIFE can place challenges right at your feet.
LIFE can make good of the hardships we meet.
LIFE can overwhelm you and make your head spin.
LIFE can reward those determined to win.
LIFE can be hurtful and not always fair.
LIFE can surround you with people who care.
LIFE clearly does offer its ups and its downs.
LIFE's days can bring you both smiles and frowns.
LIFE teaches us to take the good with the bad.
LIFE is a mixture of happy and sad.

SO...

Take the life that you have and give it your best.
Think positive be happy let God do the rest.
Take the challenges that life has laid at your feet.
Take pride and be thankful for each one you meet.
To yourself give forgiveness if you stumble and fall.
Take each day that is dealt you and give it your all.
Take the love that you're given and return it with care.
Have faith that when needed it will always be there.
Take time to find the beauty in the things that you see.
Take life's simple pleasures let them set your heart free.
The idea here is simply to even the score.
As you are met and faced with Life's Tug of War.

CG

I ARISE TODAY THROUGH THE STRENGTH OF HEAVEN; LIGHT OF THE SUN, SPLENDOR OF FIRE, SPEED OF LIGHTNING, SWIFTNESS OF THE WIND, DEPTH OF THE SEA, STABILITY OF THE EARTH, FIRMNESS OF THE ROCK. I ARISE TODAY

Extract from The Prayer of St Patrick

☙

Have no fear *Robin Jarvis*

"Have no fear," the voice told her,
"for in thee lies the hope of all.
Only thou can deliver the land from darkness."
"How can I?" she asked. "I am just one against so many."
The eyes gleamed behind the dappling leaves.
"Yet the smallest acorn may become the tallest oak,"
came the answer.

The Swallow

...and perhaps
Morgan Harper Nichols

"and perhaps
what made her beautiful
was not her appearance
or what she achieved,
but in her love
and in her courage,
and her audacity
to believe:
no matter
the darkness
around her,
Light ran wild
within her,
and that was the way
she came alive,
and it showed up
in everything."

ᘉ

When I am Down...
Brendan Graham

When I am down and oh, my soul, so weary
When troubles come and my heart burdened be
And I am still and wait here in the silence
Until you come and sit a while with me

You raise me up, so I can stand on mountains
You raise me up, to walk on stormy seas
I am strong, when I am on your shoulders
You raise me up, to more than I can be

*In the depth of winter
I finally learned
that there was in me
an invincible summer*

Albert Camus

The Swallow

One Last Conversation *Anon*

'One last conversation
So much to say.
So little actually said.
But the pills, the piles of sympathetic letters,
the constant flow of visitors said it all

We chat, we gossip, we exchange insights about our shared world.
I'm too British, too male, too stiff upper-lipped to really talk about the fact
that it's a world you and I both know you'll soon be leaving
To talk about the fact that your "battle" is almost at an end
You "fought" they said.
You've been so "brave" they said
Yet you know, I know, anyone who has faced it knows differently
Cancer is not a battle.

There is no choice whether to fight let alone whether to win or lose.
No amount of courage no measure of cowardice can decide the outcome.
There is no virtue in survival. Certainly no lack of it in death.
I lived.
You now know that you will not.
Luck. Chance. Fate. Nothing more. Nothing less.
You didn't ...couldn't choose
You didn't ...couldn't decide.
Save, that is, for one thing.
You chose to confront your sickness, your pain, your fear in public
Your decision made thousands realise they were not alone
That really was brave. That a choice that let others know that their sickness,
their pain and their fear was not, in fact, just theirs
That one last conversation which was so very worthwhile having.
As I leave you gripped my arm. An unspoken goodbye.
Only now do I know what I should have said.
No one who heard you talk about what you've faced will ever forget
Oh yes and one more thing.
Thank you.'

I say this because with every step I take
I am scared of falling
but it is this fear that makes me
work harder to make sure I don't fall.

Paul Breen

☙

A Reminder from Smaller Beings *by Nikita Gill*

The bird building her home on your windowsill
has had every nest destroyed before.
The spider that is delicately weaving a silken masterpiece
has had every single thread broken before.
And despite it all,
they try again.

☙

"OH YES, THE PAST CAN HURT. BUT
THE WAY I SEE IT, YOU CAN EITHER
RUN FROM IT, OR... LEARN FROM IT."

Rafiki, The Lion King

March 22nd 2010 – a day I shall never forget *Paul Breen, 2021*

March 22nd 2010 is a day I shall never forget.
I was driving a train from Glasgow to Aberdeen.
We went through a tunnel. I coughed very lightly and immediately felt
what was like a rush of water going up the back of my head.
I knew I was in trouble so quickly called the conductor to tell him that I
was going to have to stop the train once through the tunnel.
I managed to stop the train at the next signal, knowing that the emergency
services would be able to find me easily. At this stage my left weight was a
dead weight and my left arm was swinging about uncontrollably.
2 off duty nurses, one dentist and a first aider stayed with me until a
paramedic arrived.
I remember the ambulance doors opening and no more.

My next memory was being asked my name, date of birth and did I know
where I was to which I replied "Hospital in Glasgow" I was actually in
Aberdeen Royal Infirmary where I had been for a week, following a stay
in three different hospitals in Glasgow. I have no memory of any of them.
After many months in Aberdeen Royal Infirmary I was moved to Neuro
Rehab to get me strong enough to return home.

During my time in rehab, I developed a build-up of blood on my brain.
My surgeon told me that an operation would give me a 50/50 chance
of survival. Following the operation unfortunately I suffered severe
complications. I remember having one operation but my family tell me I
had 14 operations.

I was flown down to Papworth hospital where I spent 5 weeks of which
I remember barely anything. From there I spent a week in Addenbrookes
hospital but I became so critically unwell that I was flown back to
Aberdeen Royal Infirmary.

My wife told me that this was the darkest period of my hospital stays. On
4 separate occasions my family were called in to be told that I was not
expected to survive the night. My wife and I had always hoped to renew

our wedding vows. She held my hand whilst one of the hospital chaplains blessed her wedding ring. When he left the room, I opened my eyes. From here on I went from strength to strength thanks to the incredible nursing staff on the ward. I was referred to as The Miracle Man.

Apparently, only 1 in 3 people worldwide survive what I had been through. I never refused a workout, and the physios came to me every time they had a No Show, so I was able to push myself further.

I was moved to the rehabilitation unit and it was whilst sitting in the garden there that it hit me hard just how much I wanted to go home. in order to do so I needed to double my physical efforts by asking to spend longer on the treadmill etc. whilst speaking to the physio, she suggested that I set myself the challenge of walking a mile for Sport Relief. I completed this task and in doing so I managed to raise a significant amount for charity thanks to my physio cajoling so many other members of staff into sponsoring me

During my stay in hospital the Chaplain paid me a visit. I told him that he should not bother wasting his time with me as I hadn't a religious bone in my body to which he suggested that he visit me as a friend instead. I looked forward to his visits. We became friends. He is quite a character, with a wonderful sense of humour.

I will always be indebted to those who cared for me in hospital, the NHS staff, and to those friends who visited me including my Railway colleagues, my boys and my family. My wife gave up her life for me, visiting twice daily no matter where I was. She sat by my bedside, holding my hand, singing songs and telling me stories. She never gave up on me. Quite simply, she is my Rock.

In conclusion, I was discharged from hospital 2 yrs and 29 days after I was taken ill. Although my health is still very much fragile and I suffer multiple health problems, but having seen so many others suffering from

The Swallow

severe neurological problems and feeling as though I have been physically hammered, compared to others I met along my hospital journey, I feel lucky to be alive.

The one song that inspired me when I was stuck in my hospital bed was a song by Katy Perry called Firework and if you listen carefully to the lyrics am sure you would understand why.

> *You don't have to feel like a waste of space*
> *You're original, cannot be replaced*
> *If you only knew what the future holds*
> *After a hurricane comes a rainbow*
> *Maybe a reason why all the doors are closed*
> *So you could open one that leads you to the perfect road*
> *Like a lightning bolt, your heart will glow*
> *And when it's time, you'll know*
> *Cause baby, you're a firework*
> *Come on, show them what you're worth*

03

"We have been called to heal wounds, to unite what has fallen apart, and to bring home those who have lost their way."

St Francis of Assisi

O my God, teach me to receive *St Ignatius*

O my God, teach me to receive
the sick in your name. Give to
my efforts success for the glory
of your holy name.
It is your work: without you,
I cannot succeed.
Grant that the sick you have
placed in my care may be
abundantly blessed, and not
one of them be lost because
of any neglect on my part.
Help me to overcome, every
temporal weakness, and
strengthen in me whatever
may enable me to bring joy
to the lives of those I serve.
Give me grace, for the sake of
your sick ones and of those lives
that will be influenced by them.
AMEN.

03

"...as the slow sea sucked at the shore and then withdrew, leaving
the strip of seaweed bare and the shingle churned, the sea birds
raced and ran upon the beaches. Then that same impulse to flight
seized upon them too. Crying, whistling, calling, they skimmed
the placid sea and left the shore. Make haste, make speed, hurry
and begone; yet where, and to what purpose? The restless urge
of autumn, unsatisfying, sad, had put a spell upon them and they
must flock, and wheel, and cry; they must spill themselves of
motion before winter came."

Daphne du Maurier

...to die will be an awfully big adventure.

J.M. Barrie, Peter Pan

ℭℨ

A giant pine, magnificent and old... *Georgia Harkness*

A giant pine, magnificent and old
Stood staunch against the sky and all around
Shed beauty, grace and power. Within its fold birds safely
reared their young.
The velvet ground beneath was gentle,
and the cooling shade gave cheer to passers by.
Its towering arms a landmark stood, erect and unafraid,
As if to say, "Fear naught from life's alarms".
It fell one day. Where it had dauntless stood was loneliness
and void.
But men who passed paid tribute – and said,
 "To know this life was good,
 It left its mark on me. Its work stands fast".
 And so it lives. Such life no bonds can hold –
 This giant pine, magnificent and old.

Life is like a Round of Golf *Criswell Freeman*

Life is like a round of golf
With many a turn and twist.
But the game is much too sweet and short
To curse the shots you've missed.
Sometimes you'll hit it straight and far
Sometimes the putts roll true.
But each round has it's errant shots
And troubles to play through.
So always swing with courage
No matter what the lie.
And never let the hazards
Destroy the joy inside.
And keep a song within your heart
Give thanks that you can play.
For the round is much too short and sweet
To let it slip away.

Ↄ

When your Child Dies *Hanya Yanagihara*

"...when your child dies, you feel everything you'd expect to feel,
feelings so well-documented by so many others that I won't even bother to
list them here, except to say that everything that's written about mourning
is all the same, and it's all the same for a reason – because there is no read
deviation from the text. Sometimes you feel more of one thing and less of
another, and sometimes you feel them out of order, and sometimes you feel
them for a longer time or a shorter time.

But the sensations are always the same. But here's what no one says – when
it's your child, a part of you, a very tiny but nonetheless unignorable part of
you, also feels relief. Because finally, the moment you have been expecting,
been dreading, been preparing yourself for since the day you became a
parent, has come. Ah, you tell yourself, it's arrived.

Here it is. And after that, you have nothing to fear again."

The Impossible Dream Poem *Joe Darion*

To dream the impossible dream
To fight the unbeatable foe
To bear with unbearable sorrow
To run where the brave dare not go

To right the unrightable wrong
To love pure and chaste from afar
To try when your arms are too weary
To reach the unreachable star

This is my quest
To follow that star
No matter how hopeless
No matter how far

To fight for the right
Without question or pause
To be willing to march into hell
For a heavenly cause

And I know if I'll only be true
To this glorious quest
That my heart will lie peaceful and calm
When I'm laid to my rest

And the world will be better for this
That one man, scorned and covered with scars
Still strove with his last ounce of courage
To reach the unreachable star

ભ

If you don't let it out, the grief becomes a scream trapped inside your soul, a constant cry in the dark, a sob you can never release. So scream, shout, cry, the way the sky does with thunder and lightning and rain… for it knows it is being cleansed, it knows that its storm is the only way to release the pain. *Nikita Gill*

Crabbit Old Woman *Phyllis McCormack*

What do you see, nurse, what do you see?
What are you thinking, when you look at me?

A crabbit old woman, not very wise,
Uncertain of habit, with far-away eyes,
Who dribbles her food and makes no reply
When you say in a loud voice, I do wish you'd try.

Who seems not to notice the things that you do
And forever is losing a stocking or shoe.
Who, unresisting or not; lets you do as you will
With bathing and feeding the long day is fill.

Is that what you're thinking, Is that what you see?
Then open your eyes, nurse, you're looking at me.
I'll tell you who I am as I sit here so still!
As I rise at your bidding, as I eat at your will.

I'm a small child of 10 with a father and mother,
Brothers and sisters, who loved one another
A young girl of 16 with wings on her feet,
Dreaming that soon now a lover she'll meet,

A bride soon at 20 - my heart gives a leap,
Recalling the vows that I promised to keep.
At 25 now I have young of my own
Who need me to build a secure happy home;

A woman of 30, my young now grow fast,
Bound to each other with ties that should last;

At 40, my young sons have grown and are gone,
But my man is beside me to see I don't mourn;

At 50 once more babies play around my knee,
Again we know children, my loved one and me.

Dark days are upon me, my husband is dead,
I look at the future, I shudder with dread,
For my young are all rearing young ones of their own.
And I think of the years and the love that I've known;

I'm an old woman now and nature is cruel,
Tis her jest to make old age look like a fool.
The body is crumbled, grace and vigor depart,
There is now a stone where I once had a heart,

But inside this old carcass, a young girl still dwells,
And now and again my battered heart swells,
I remember the joy, I remember the pain,
And I'm loving and living life over again.

I think of the years all too few, gone too fast.
And accept the stark fact that nothing can last
So open your eyes, nurse, open and see,
Not a crabbit old woman, look closer-
See Me.

ℭℨ

A Nurse's reply "To the 'Crabbit Old Woman"

What do we see, you ask, what do we see?
Yes, we are thinking when looking at thee!

We may seem to be hard when we hurry and fuss,
But there's many of you, and too few of us.

...*continued*

The Swallow

We would like far more time to sit by you and talk,
To bath you and feed you and help you to walk.

To hear of your lives and the things you have done,
Your childhood, your husband, your daughter, your son.

But time is against us, there's too much
Patients too many, and nurses too few.

We grieve when we see you so sad and alone,
With nobody near you, no friends of your own.

We feel all your pain, and know of your fear
That nobody cares now your end is so near.

But nurses are people with feelings as well,
And when we're together you'll often hear tell

Of the dearest old Gran in the very end bed,
And the lovely old Dad, and the things that he said,

We speak with compassion and love, and feel sad
When we think of your lives and the joy that you've had,

When the time has arrived for you to depart,
You leave us behind with an ache in our heart.

When you sleep the long sleep, no more worry or care,
There are other old people, and we must be there.

So please understand if we hurry and fuss –
There are many of you,

And so few of us.

EVERY STRUGGLE IN
YOUR LIFE WILL BECOME
A STORY SOMEDAY.
IT WILL EITHER BE A
STORY ABOUT HOW
YOU GOT STRONGER
AND PERSEVERED OR A
STORY ABOUT WHY YOU
GAVE UP. YOU CAN'T
ALWAYS CHOOSE YOUR
STRUGGLES BUT YOU CAN
CHOOSE WHICH STORY
BECOMES TRUE.

David Willis

The Swallow

When You Meet Someone Deep In Grief
by Partricia McKernon Runkle

Slip off your shoes
and set them by the door.

Enter barefoot
this darkened chapel,

hollowed by loss,
hallowed by sorrow,

its grey stone walls
and floor.

You, congregation
of one

are here to listen,
not to sing.

Kneel in the back pew,
make no sound.

Let the candles
speak.

❧

*Our greatest weakness lies in giving up.
The most certain way to succeed
is always to try just one more time.*

Thomas Edison

Courage doesn't always roar.
Sometimes courage is the quiet voice
at the end of the day saying, (whispering),
"I will try again tomorrow"   *Mary Anne Ryder*

ⳤ

The Oak Tree *Jonny Ray Ryder*

A mighty wind blew night and day
It stole the oak tree's leaves away
Then snapped its boughs and pulled its bark
Until the oak was tired and stark

But still the oak tree held its ground
While other trees fell all around
The weary wind gave up and spoke.
"How can you still be standing Oak?"

The oak tree said, "I know that you
Can break each branch of mine in two
Carry every leaf away
Shake my limbs, and make me sway

But I have roots stretched in the earth
Growing stronger since my birth
You'll never touch them, for you see
They are the deepest part of me

Until today, I wasn't sure
Of just how much I could endure
But now I've found, with thanks to you
I'm stronger than I ever knew."

A Mother's Grief *Anon*

You ask me how I'm feeling,
but do you really want to know?
The moment I try telling you,
you say you have to go.

How can I tell you,
what it's been like for me.
I am haunted, I am broken
by things that you don't see.

You ask me how I'm holding up,
but do you really care?
The second I try to speak my heart,
you start squirming in your chair.

Because I am so lonely,
you see, no one comes around,
I'll take the words I want to say
and quietly choke them down.

Everyone avoids me now,
because they don't know what to say
They tell me I'll be there for you,
then turn and walk away.

Call me if you need me,
that's what everybody said,
But how can I call you
and scream into the phone, my child is dead.

No one will let me say the words
I need to say
Why does a mothers grief
scare everyone away?

I am tired of pretending
as my heart pounds in my chest,
I say things to make you comfortable,
but my soul finds no rest.

How can I tell you things,
that are too sad to be told,
of the helplessness I feel inside
I am too afraid to be bold.

If you really love me,
and I believe you do,
if you really want to help me,
here is what I need from you.

Sit down beside me,
reach out and take my hand,
Say "My friend, I've come to listen,
I want to understand."

Just hold my hand and listen
that's all you need to do,
And if by chance I shed a tear,
it's alright if you do too.

☙

YOU NEVER KNOW
HOW STRONG YOU ARE
UNTIL BEING STRONG IS THE
ONLY CHOICE YOU HAVE. *Bob Marley*

A Father's Grief *Anon*

It must be very difficult
To be a man in grief,
Since "men don't cry" and "men are strong",
No tears can bring relief.

It must be very difficult
To stand up to the test,
And field the calls and visitors
So she can get some rest.

They always ask if she's alright
And what she's going through.
But seldom take his hand and ask,
"My friend, but how are you?"

He hears her crying in the night
And thinks his heart will break.
He dries her tears and comforts her,
But "stays strong" for her sake.

It must be very difficult
To start each day anew.
And try to be so very brave–
He lost his child too.

ɔ3

*The song is ended
but the melody lingers on*

Irving Berlin

You Start Dying Slowly *Pablo Neruda*

You start dying slowly
if you do not travel,
if you do not read,
If you do not listen to the sounds of life,
If you do not appreciate yourself.

You start dying slowly
When you kill your self-esteem;
When you do not let others help you.

You start dying slowly
If you become a slave of your habits,
Walking every day on the same paths…
If you do not change your routine,
If you do not wear different colours
Or you do not speak to those you don't know.

You start dying slowly
If you avoid to feel passion
And their turbulent emotions;
Those which make your eyes glisten
And your heart beat fast.

You start dying slowly
If you do not change your life when you are not satisfied with your job,
or with your love,
If you do not risk what is safe for the uncertain,

If you do not go after a dream,
If you do not allow yourself,
At least once in your lifetime,
To run away from sensible advice.

The Old Song *Charles Kingsley (1819–1875)*

When all the world is young, lad,
        And all the trees are green;
And every goose a swan, lad,
        And every lass a queen;
Then hey for boot and horse, lad,
        And round the world away!
Young blood must have its course, lad,
        And every dog his day.

When all the world is old, lad,
        And all the trees are brown;
And all the sport is stale, lad,
        And all the wheels run down;
Creep home, and take your place there
        The spent and maim'd among;
God grant you find one face there
        You loved when all was young!

cs

You cannot die of grief, though it feels as if you can. A heart does not actually break, though sometimes your chest aches as if it is breaking. Grief dims with time. It is the way of things. There comes a day when you smile again, and you feel like a traitor. How dare I feel happy. How dare I be glad in a world where my father is no more. And then you cry fresh tears, because you do not miss him as much as you once did, and giving up your grief is another kind of death.   *Laurell K. Hamilton*

I Have Walked that Long Road to Freedom
Nelson Mandela

"I have walked that long road to freedom. I have tried not to falter; I have made missteps along the way. But I have discovered the secret that after climbing a great hill, one only finds that there are many more hills to climb. I have taken a moment here to rest, to steal a view of the glorious vista that surrounds me, to look back on the distance I have come. But I can only rest for a moment, for with freedom come responsibilities, and I dare not linger, for my long walk is not ended."

ᴄʒ

Fear is the greatest obstacle to learning. But fear is your best friend. Fear is like fire. If you learn to control it, you let it work for you. If you don't learn to control it, it'll destroy you and everything around you.

Cus D'Amato

The Swallow

For me, trees have always been the most penetrating preachers
Hermann Hesse

For me, trees have always been the most penetrating preachers. I revere them when they live in tribes and families, in forests and groves. And even more, I revere them when they stand alone. They are like lonely persons. Not like hermits who have stolen away out of some weakness, but like great, solitary men, like Beethoven and Nietzsche. In their highest boughs the world rustles, their roots rest in infinity; but they do not lose themselves there, they struggle with all the force of their lives for one thing only: to fulfil themselves according to their own laws, to build up their own form, to represent themselves. Nothing is holier, nothing is more exemplary than a beautiful, strong tree. When a tree is cut down and reveals its naked death-wound to the sun, one can read its whole history in the luminous, inscribed disk of its trunk: in the rings of its years, its scars, all the struggle, all the suffering, all the sickness, all the happiness and prosperity stand truly written, the narrow years and the luxurious years, the attacks withstood, the storms endured. And every young farm boy knows that the hardest and noblest wood has the narrowest rings, that high on the mountains and in continuing danger the most indestructible, the strongest, the ideal trees grow.

Trees are sanctuaries. Whoever knows how to speak to them, whoever knows how to listen to them, can learn the truth. They do not preach learning and precepts, they preach, undeterred by particulars, the ancient law of life.

A tree says: A kernel is hidden in me, a spark, a thought, I am life from eternal life. The attempt and the risk that the eternal mother took with me is unique, unique the form and veins of my skin, unique the smallest play of leaves in my branches and the smallest scar on my bark. I was made to form and reveal the eternal in my smallest special detail.

A tree says: My strength is trust. I know nothing about my fathers, I know nothing about the thousand children that every year spring out of me. I live out the secret of my seed to the very end, and I care for nothing else. I trust that God is in me. I trust that my labor is holy. Out of this trust I live.

When we are stricken and cannot bear our lives any longer, then a tree has something to say to us: Be still! Be still! Look at me! Life is not easy, life is not difficult. Those are childish thoughts. Let God speak within you, and your thoughts will grow silent. You are anxious because your path leads away from mother and home. But every step and every day lead you back again to the mother. Home is neither here nor there. Home is within you, or home is nowhere at all.

A longing to wander tears my heart when I hear trees rustling in the wind at evening. If one listens to them silently for a long time, this longing reveals its kernel, its meaning. It is not so much a matter of escaping from one's suffering, though it may seem to be so. It is a longing for home, for a memory of the mother, for new metaphors for life. It leads home. Every path leads homeward, every step is birth, every step is death, every grave is mother.

So the tree rustles in the evening, when we stand uneasy before our own childish thoughts: Trees have long thoughts, long-breathing and restful, just as they have longer lives than ours. They are wiser than we are, as long as we do not listen to them. But when we have learned how to listen to trees, then the brevity and the quickness and the childlike hastiness of our thoughts achieve an incomparable joy. Whoever has learned how to listen to trees no longer wants to be a tree. He wants to be nothing except what he is. That is home. That is happiness.

ଓ

You always had the power my dear, you just had to learn it for yourself *Glinda, The Wizard of Oz*

I honestly mean it when I say
I am grateful that I had a tumour... *Lucia Cioffi 2022*

I honestly mean it when I say I am grateful that I had a tumour as it led me to meet such wonderful altruistic people who put so many others first and are willing to share part of their life journey with us.

I was diagnosed with a brain tumour back in October 2021 and from the minute I stepped into the office to meet my neurologist and Neurosurgeon in the ARI Neuroscience ward, I immediately knew I was going to be in good hands. My neurologist actually took my hand and silently imparted all the encouragement and support he could through that small gesture (even though he has only seen me through a video call once before).

Two weeks later I had a 10-hour surgery to remove my tentorial meningioma (amazing how much I know about the brain now... lol) – I woke up hours later and for 2 days everyone was upside down, luckily I was heavily sedated as it was quite freakish, glad that didn't last long and developed into double vision and morning consultations seemed to have 20 odd people in them – made me feel important!

Infection followed and a 3-month stay in ward 205 (short time compared to others) but I am finally home. Being looked after by the staff there has given me an entirely new perspective on what it means to really care about your fellow human being. I have made lots of new friends and like the song says I was a little sad to leave. During my time there I crocheted a brain beanie for Mr. Bodkin who is a top Surgeon and Lead consultant but despite how high up he is he honestly never minded putting on the beanie and came to say goodbye to me, wearing it, on the day I left. Supracerebellarinfratentorialmeningioma really put a smile on the staff's faces so much so that Claire McNab, Amy from Physio, Mr. Bodkin, nurses, and more did a little dance with sick bowls as hats to say goodbye (a sendoff that makes me smile).

I even heard that staff were wheeling a patient down to theatre and singing "into theatre, snip away" Prior to this I suffered from severe clinical depression and listened to a chap on YouTube called Douglas Bloch, he introduced his followers to the phrase "All will be well" by Julian of Norwich. This kind of became a mantra between Robert (my partner) and I. During the long nights and horrendous pain of the past 3 months "All will be well" became more than words and is a line that comforts and brings hope no matter what happens, Life is a climb but All will be well.

Supercerebellar infratentorial meningioma

If you treat it soon enough you won't be in a coma
And if you get the Bodkin Team it won't be too much bother
Supercerebellar infratentorial meningioma

Into the theatre snip away
Into the theatre snip away
Into the theatre snip away
Into the theatre snip away

I went to see my GP with a throbbing in my head
And after MRIs and things this is what they said,
"You'll need to come for resection, we're finding you a bed"
Then surgeons bravely took the path where angels fear to tread.

Oh... Supercerebellar infratentorial meningioma
If you treat it soon enough you won't be in a coma
And if you get the Bodkin Team it won't be too much bother
Supercerebellar infratentorial meningioma

Into the theatre snip away
Into the theatre snip away
Into the theatre snip away
Into the theatre snip away

The team that they assembled was the top team in the land
The artistry of resection was the best of skillful hands
And all the care from all the staff meant I could then withstand
The rocky road to freedom from the tumour's one last stand

Oh...
Supercerebellar infratentorial meningioma
If you treat it soon enough you won't be in a coma
And if you get the Bodkin Team it won't be too much bother
Supracerebellar infratentorial meningioma

Into the theatre snip away
Into the theatre snip away
You know you can say it *backward and that would be,
Emm, oh dear, never mind…

Villainous Staph Aurius tried to make it all go bad
But intravenous anti-Bs rode in like Sir Galahad
So now it's time to be discharged, I feel a little sad
But hooray they've got me back to health and my normal
kind of "mad"

*Backward is: gioma menin tentorial infra cerebellar supra
All will be well.

☙

TODAY HAS NOT BEEN A FAILURE BECAUSE TOMORROW IS ANOTHER DAY TO SUCCEED!

You rest in the arms of angels
In a place of peace and love
Watching over me always
From heaven up above.

You guide me through my worries
And help me through each day
Always by my side
You never went away.

The bond cannot be broken
Made from love so pure
Death does not break the bond
It lives on for ever more.

You rest in the arms of angels
Free from illness and pain
Waiting for the day
We are together once again.

John F Connor

The Swallow

**Every month Martín's parents took a trip
to see Grandma...**
Anon

Every month Martín's parents took a trip to see Grandma and came home on the same train the next day.

One day the child said to his parents:

I'm already grown up.
Can I go to my grandma's alone?

After a brief discussion, his parents accepted.

They stood with him as he waited for the train to exit.

They said goodbye to their son and gave him some tips through the window.

Martin repeated to them:

I know. I've been told this more than a thousand times.

As the train was about to leave, his father murmured in his ear:

Son if you feel bad or insecure, this is for you!

And he put something in his pocket.

Now Martin was alone,
sitting on the train as he had wanted,
without his parents for the first time.

He was admiring the landscape out the window.
Around him some unknowns pushed themselves in.
They made a lot of noise.

They got in and out of the train car.

The conductor made some comments about him being alone.

One person looked at him with eyes of sadness.

Martin was feeling more uneasy with
every minute that passed.
And now he was scared.

He felt cornered and alone.
He put his head down, and
with tears in his eyes,
He remembered his dad had
Put something in his pocket.
Trembling, he searched for what his father had given him.

Upon finding the piece of paper he read it:

Son, I'm in the last train car!

That's how life is,
We must let our kids go
We must let them try new things.

But we always like to be
In the last car, watching,
in case they are afraid
or in case they find obstacles and don't know what to do.

We want to be close to them.
as long as we are still alive.

When God Created Woman *Donna Ashworth*

When God created woman he was working late on the 6th day...
An angel came by and asked. "Why spend so much time on her?"
The lord answered. "Have you seen all the specifications I have to meet to shape her?"
She must function on all kinds of situations,
She must be able to embrace several kids at the same time,
Have a hug that can heal anything from a bruised knee to a broken heart,
She must do all this with only two hands,"She cures herself when sick and can work 18 hours a day"
The Angel was impressed "Just two hands... impossible!
And this is the standard model?"
The Angel came closer and touched the woman
"But you have made her so soft, Lord".
"She is soft", said the Lord,
"But I have made her strong. You can't imagine what she can endure and overcome."
"Can she think?" The Angel asked...
The Lord answered. "Not only can she think, she can reason and negotiate."
The Angel touched her cheek...
"Lord, it seems this creation is leaking! You have put too many burdens on her"
"She is not leaking... it is a tear" The Lord corrected the Angel...
"What's it for?" Asked the Angel.
The Lord said. "Tears are her way of expressing her grief, her doubts, her love, her loneliness, her suffering and her pride."...
This made a big impression on the Angel,
"Lord, you are a genius. You thought of everything.
A woman is indeed marvellous"
Lord said. "Indeed she is.
She has strength that amazes a man.
She can handle trouble and carry heavy burdens.
She holds happiness, love and opinions.

She smiles when she feels like screaming.
She sings when she feels like crying, cries when happy and laughs when afraid.
She fights for what she believes in.
Her love is unconditional.
Her heart is broken when a next-of-kin or a friend dies but she finds strength to get on with life"
The Angel asked: "So she is a perfect being?"
The lord replied: "No. She has just one drawback
She often forgets what she is worth."

cs

With him, life was routine; without him, life was unbearable

Harper Lee

The Swallow

Thoughts from a Paramedic

You walk back into the station after booking onto the Ambulance ready for what the day brings. You and your crew mate, colleague, friend and even the one that gets on your nerves. You have a little banter debate as to who is putting the kettle on and making the brews. Past days, nights, days off and home life are spoke about between you both and bekng a family you listen intently with laughter, interest and compassion. The brews are made and you head for the comfy seat bashing each other as you go – like when you fight the old lady in the supermarket for the last bag of potatoes – for who gets the comfiest seat. You sit down victorious and start bringing that delicious hot beverage to your lips... SUDDENLY the radios scream into life, you recognise the radio code, unfortunately you've attended too many in the past while... it's an RTC.

You immediately drop all and start heading for the ambulance knowing full well that somewhere someone needs you in that fire moment, you climb into the battle bus and as whoever is driving gets moving you read the screen aloud so your colleague and friend is up to date as well. As you read the screen you get a feeling of what your heading too (not always accurate), you start getting prepped wether it being putting on high-vis clothing and helmet or getting in your 'time to work' frame of mind. Traffic is heavy but you make good progress trying not to use pub language for the vehicles that somehow can't see or hear you, you turn the corner and see your destination... CARNAGE.

You stop and get to work doing what we do best whilst chaos ensues around you but your focused on your patient, inside you cannot wait to hear the siren screams of approaching backup ambulances, police and even the water fairies – knowing full well that things are going to get a lot better real soon, many hands make light work etc. They arrive and suddenly time almost slows as the hussle and bustle of all these amazing people do what they do and suddenly trapped casualties are extricated, the roads are closed and safe, your back in your second home and doing all you can to make sure your patient gets to go home to their family.

This time it's a good outcome for all, the person you didn't know existed before and now have seen in their birthday suit has been handed over to the awaiting hospital and you head back to clean and sort the ambulance. All of a sudden the organised chaos is over and an eerie silence and calm envelopes your immediate world. During the cleaning and sorting you and your crew mate and friend discuss the events and wonder HOW it's been a good outcome after witnessing the scene but you don't care how or why you just thank whoever it is you thank that it's a good outcome.

You press clear and start making the journey to home station, times are pumping out the radio and the banter and nerve stepping slowly reappears, things are good when suddenly the screen screams into life... NO ...another one, then suddenly the radio squawks into life and control say words no one should have to endure... no pulse no breathing. Here we go again...

CB

If you think you are too small to make a difference you obviously haven't spent the night with a mosquito

Dare to Be

WHEN a new day begins, dare to smile gratefully.
WHEN there is darkness, dare to be the first to shine a light.
WHEN there is injustice, dare to be the first to condemn it.
WHEN something seems difficult, dare to do it anyway.
WHEN life seems to beat you down, dare to fight back.
WHEN there seems to be no hope, dare to find some.
WHEN you're feeling tired, dare to keep going.
WHEN times are tough, dare to be tougher.
WHEN love hurts you, dare to love again.
WHEN someone is hurting, dare to help them heal.
WHEN another is lost, dare to help them find the way.
WHEN a friend falls, dare to be the first to extend a hand.
WHEN you cross paths with another, dare to make them smile.
WHEN you feel great, dare to help someone else feel great too.
WHEN the day has ended, dare to feel as you've done your best.
DARE to be the best you can –
At all times, DARE TO BE!

ର

Write it on your heart that every day is the best day
in the year.
He is rich who owns the day, and no one owns the day
who allows it to be invaded with fret and anxiety.

Finish every day and be done with it.
You have done what you could.
Some blunders and absurdities, no doubt crept in.
Forget them as soon as you can, tomorrow is a new day;
begin it well and serenely, with too high a spirit
to be cumbered with your old nonsense.

This new day is too dear, with its hopes and invitations,
to waste a moment on the yesterdays.

GOD USES BROKEN THINGS. IT TAKES
BROKEN SOIL TO PRODUCE A CROP,
BROKEN CLOUDS TO GIVE RAIN,
BROKEN GRAIN TO GIVE BREAD,
BROKEN BREAD TO GIVE STRENGTH.

Vance Havner

☙

Mighty Oak *Kathy J Parenteau*

Stand tall, oh mighty oak, for all the world to see.
Your strength and undying beauty forever amazes me.
Though storm clouds hover above you,
Your branches span the sky
In search of the radiant sunlight you
Count on to survive.
When the winds are high and restless and
You lose a limb or two,
It only makes you stronger.
We could learn so much from you.
Though generations have come and gone
And brought about such change,
Quietly you've watched them all,
Yet still remained the same.
I only pray God gives to me
The strength he's given you
To face each day with hope,
Whether skies are black or blue.
Life on earth is truly a gift.
Every moment we must treasure.
It's the simple things we take for granted
That become our ultimate pleasures.

The Swallow

Emergency Medical Services Prayer

As I perform my duty Lord
Whatever be the call,
Help to guide and keep me safe
From dangers big and small.
I want to serve and do my best
No matter what the scene,
I pledge to keep my skills refined,
My judgment quick and keen.
This calling to give of my self
Most do not understand,
But I stand ready all the time
To help my fellow man.
To have the chance to help a child
Restore his laugh with glee,
A word of thanks I might not hear,
But knowing is enough for me.
The praise of men is fine for some,
But I feel truly blessed,
That you oh Lord have chosen me
To serve in EMS!

⅓

There's going to be... *Erin Van Vuren*

There's going to be very painful moments in your life
that will change your entire world in a matter of minutes.
These moments will change you.
Let them make you stronger, smarter, and kinder.
Don't you go and become someone that you're not.
Cry.
Scream if you have to.
Then you straighten out that crown
and keep it moving.

Because in the end,
you won't remember the time
you spent working in the office
or mowing your lawn.
Climb that goddamn mountain

Jack Kerouac

ଓଃ

You'll Never Walk Alone
Rodgers & Hammerstein

When you walk through a storm
hold your head up high
And don't be afraid of the dark
At the end of a storm is a golden sky
And the sweet silver song of a lark

Walk on through the wind
Walk on through the rain
Tho' your dreams
Be tossed and blown
Walk on
Walk on
With hope in your heart
And you'll never walk alone
You'll never walk alone

The Swallow

I Never Can Do It *Katherine Pyle*

"I never can do it," the little kite said,
As he looked at the others high over his head;
"I know I should fall if I tried to fly."
"Try," said the big kite; "only try!
Or I fear you never will learn at all."

But the little kite said, "I'm afraid I'll fall."
The big kite nodded: "Ah well, goodbye;
I'm off" and he rose toward the tranquil sky.

Then the little kite's paper stirred at the sight,
And trembling he shook himself free for flight.
First, whirling and frightened, then braver grown,
Up, up he rose through the air alone,
Till the big kite looking down could see
The little one rising steadily.

Then how the little kite thrilled with pride,
As he sailed with the big kite side by side!
While far below he could see the ground,
And the boys like small spots moving round.

They rested high in the quiet air,
And only the birds and the clouds were there.
"Oh, how happy I am!" the little kite cried,
"And all because I was brave, and tried."

%

It is not the mountain we conquer but ourselves

Edmund Hillary

The Poppy *Paul Hunter*

I am not a badge of honour,
I am not a racist smear,
I am not a fashion statement,
To be worn but once a year,
I am not glorification
Of conflict or of war.
I am not a paper ornament
A token,
I am more.
I am a loving memory,
Of a father or a son,
A permanent reminder
Of each and every one.
I'm paper or enamel
I'm old or shining new,
I'm a way of saying thank you,
To every one of you.
I am a simple poppy
A reminder to you all,
That courage faith and honour,
Will stand where heroes fall.

ᘓ

THERE IS NO GRIEF LIKE THE GRIEF THAT DOES NOT SPEAK

Henry Wadsworth Longfellow

Every Birth Begins a Mystery *Jennifer Worth*

Every birth begins as a mystery, an enterprise whose outcome cannot be foretold. We think, "may all be well." And all is well – almost always.

But joy is only the beginning of the journey. And we must move forward, fueled by faith.

We can decide to be happy, make much out of little, embrace the warmth of our ordinary days.

Life unfolds as a mystery. An enterprise whose outcome cannot be foretold.

We do not get what we expect. We stumble on cracks, are faced with imperfection, bonds tested and tightened. And our landscapes shift in sunshine and in shade.
There is light.
There is.

Look for it.
Look for it shining over your shoulder on the past.

It was light where you went once.
It was light where you are now.
It will be light where you will go again.

ॐ

HAVE COURAGE AND BE KIND

Kate Robertson

Dandelion *Erin Hanson*

"Hold on, hold on, hold on," they said,
"You're a dandelion in the breeze,
look what the winds of change have done to all
these autumn leaves."
"Hold on, hold on, hold on,
This big wide world is not for you,
Hold on for long enough
for the last gust to dance on through."
So I held on, held on, held on,
They said that's how you know you're strong
But not until I wilted
did I notice something wrong.
I thought holding on was bravery
But when winds of change do blow
Sometimes it's even braver still
to let go, let go, let go.

❧

I loved the boy with the utmost love
of which my soul is capable,
and he is taken from me – yet in the
agony of my spirit in surrendering
such a treasure I feel a thousand
times richer than if I had never
possessed it.

William Wordsworth

The Swallow

The Wind   *Robert Louis Stevenson*

I saw you toss the kites on high
And blow the birds about the sky;
And all around I heard you pass,
Like ladies' skirts across the grass--
O wind, a-blowing all day long,
O wind, that sings so loud a song!

I saw the different things you did,
But always you yourself you hid.
I felt you push, I heard you call,
I could not see yourself at all--
O wind, a-blowing all day long,
O wind, that sings so loud a song!

O you that are so strong and cold,
O blower, are you young or old?
Are you a beast of field and tree,
Or just a stronger child than me?
O wind, a-blowing all day long,
O wind, that sings so loud a song!

⚃

I Think It's Brave   *Lana Rafaela*

I think it's brave that you get up in the morning even if
your soul is weary and your bones ache for a rest.
I think it's brave that you keep on living even if you
don't know how to anymore.
I think it's brave that you push away the waves rolling in
every day and you decide to fight.

I know there are days when you feel like giving up,
but I think it's brave that you never do.

Don't remember me with sadness,
Don't remember me with tears,
Remember all the laughter,
We've shared throughout the years.
Now I am contented
That my life it was worthwhile,
Knowing as I passed along the way
I made somebody smile.
When you are walking
                        down the street
And you've got me on your mind,
I'm walking in your footsteps
Only half a step behind.
So please don't be unhappy
Just because I'm out of sight,
Remember that I'm with you
Each morning, noon and night.

The Swallow

Silent Tears *Emily Brooklyn*

Each day as evening starts to set
The ache builds in her chest
She knows she must go to bed
And try to get some rest.

She hugs her tear stained pillow close
When no one is around
And cries for one she loved and lost
And screams without a sound

Others see her in the day
And think she's doing well
But everyday as evening sets
She enters her own hell

Time hasn't healed her pain at all
Or quieted her fears
So every night, alone in bed
She sheds those silent tears.

☙

You aren't the things that haunt you.
You aren't the pain you feel.
You aren't defective or broken.
You're human,
you're doing the best you can,
and you have so much more
to offer the world
than the demons you're fighting.

Daniel Koepke

Grief *Gwen Flowers*

I had my own notion of grief.
I thought it was the sad time
that followed the death of someone you love
and you had to push through it
to get to the other side.
But I'm learning there is no other side,
there is no pushing through,
but rather,
there is absorption,
adjustment,
acceptance.
Grief is not something you complete
but rather, you endure.
Grief is not a task to finish
and move on,
but an element of yourself –
an alteration of your being,
a new way of seeing,
a new dimension of self.

✂

You've Just Walked On Ahead of Me *Joyce Grenfell*

And I've got to understand
You must release the ones you love
And let go of their hand.
I try and cope the best I can
But I'm missing you so much
If I could only see you
And once more feel your touch.
Yes, you've just walked on ahead of me
Don't worry I'll be fine
But now and then I swear I feel
Your hand slip into mine.

I Heard Your Voice In The Wind Today *Anon*

I heard your voice in the wind today
and I turned to see your face;
The warmth of the wind caressed me
as I stood silently in place.

I felt your touch in the sun today
as its warmth filled the sky;
I closed my eyes for your embrace
and my spirit soared high.

I saw your eyes in the window pane
as I watched the falling rain;
It seemed as each raindrop fell
it quietly said your name.

I held you close in my heart today
it made me feel complete;
You may have died... but you are not gone
you will always be a part of me.

As long as the sun shines...
the wind blows...
the rain falls...
You will live on inside of me forever
for that is all my heart knows.

ॐ

FALL SEVEN TIMES
AND STAND UP EIGHT

Japanese proverb

Some People Survive *Nikita Gill*

Some people survive and talk about it.
Some people survive and go silent.
Some people survive and create.
Everyone deals with unimaginable pain in their own
way, and everyone is entitled to that, without judgement.
So the next time you look at someone's life covetously,
remember...
you may not want to endure what they are enduring
right now, at this moment,
whilst they sit so quietly before you,
looking like a calm ocean on a sunny day.
Remember how vast the ocean's boundaries are.
Whilst somewhere the water is calm, in another place in
the very same ocean, there is a colossal storm.

ᛃ

There is a voice inside of you
That whispers all day long,
"I feel this is right for me,
I know that this is wrong."
No teacher, preacher, parent, friend
Or wise man can decide
What's right for you – just listen to
The voice that speaks inside.

Shel Silverstein

Something Told the Wild Geese   *Rachel Field*

Something told the wild geese
It was time to go,
Though the fields lay golden
Something whispered, "snow."

Leaves were green and stirring,
Berries, lustre-glossed,
But beneath warm feathers
Something cautioned, "frost."

All the sagging orchards
Steamed with amber spice,
But each wild breast stiffened
At remembered ice.

Something told the wild geese
It was time to fly,
Summer sun was on their wings,
Winter in their cry.

❧

**"It is a curious thing, the death of a loved one.
We all know that our time in this world is limited,
and that eventually all of us will end up underneath
some sheet, never to wake up. And yet it is always a
surprise when it happens to someone we know. It is
like walking up the stairs to your bedroom in the dark,
and thinking there is one more stair than there is.
Your foot falls down, through the air, and there is a
sickly moment of dark surprise as you try and read
just the way you thought of things."**

I Am With You Still *Anon*

I am with you still – I do not sleep.
I am a thousand winds that blow,
I am the diamond glints on snow,
I am the sunlight on ripened grain,
I am the gentle autumn rain.

When you awaken in the morning's hush,
I am the swift, uplifting rush
of quiet birds in circled flight.
I am the soft stars that shine at night.
Do not think of me as gone –
I am with you still – in each new dawn

&#x03;

Courage is what it takes to stand up and speak; courage is also what it takes to sit down and listen.

Winston Churchill

I Want You to be Brave Enough to Jump *Lara Flanagan*

I want you to be brave enough to jump,
so you might take the chance to fly.
I want you to be forever asking
the amazing question why.
I want you to remember who you are,
after you are told who you should be.
I want you to choose hope and happiness,
and live your life without apology

CX

YOU TAKE A NUMBER OF SMALL STEPS
WHICH YOU BELIEVE ARE RIGHT,
THINKING MAYBE TOMORROW
SOMEBODY WILL TREAT THIS AS A
DANGEROUS PROVOCATION. AND THEN
YOU WAIT. IF THERE IS NO REACTION, YOU
TAKE ANOTHER STEP: COURAGE IS ONLY
AN ACCUMULATION OF SMALL STEPS.

George Konrad

CX

Whenever you find yourself doubting... *Anon*

Whenever you find yourself doubting if you can go on,
just remember how far you've come.
Remember everything you have faced,
all the battles you have won and all the fears you have overcome.
Then raise your head high and forge on ahead,
knowing that YOU GOT THIS!

Solstice Struck by yet another sudden anniversary *Anon*

Solstice Struck by yet another sudden anniversary [how
can it be so long already?] Significant dates come and
go, create continents of memory … extended lines,
sweet harmonies, a favourite lulling melody, its complex
rhythms both distract and satisfy, confirm my lonely heart
somehow… if life is rarely simple those moments, when
they come are sweet, another island beckons – pulls me
deeper still, lets me float away

∝

*What is stronger than the human heart,
which shatters over and over, and still lives*

Rupi Kaur

∝

Do not Hesitate *Mary Oliver*

If you suddenly and unexpectedly feel joy, don't hesitate.
Give in to it. There are plenty of lives and whole towns
destroyed or about to be. We are not wise, and not very
often kind. And much can never be redeemed. Still life
has some possibility left. Perhaps this is its way of fighting
back, that sometimes something happened better than all
the riches or power in the world. It could be anything, but
very likely you notice it in the instant when love begins.
Anyway, that's often the case. Anyway, whatever it is, don't
be afraid of its plenty. Joy is not made to be a crumb.

The Swallow

They say there is a reason *Anon*

They say there is a reason,
They say that time will heal,
But neither time nor reason,
Will change the way I feel,
For no-one knows the heartache,
That lies behind our smiles,
No-one knows how many times,
We have broken down and cried,
We want to tell you something,
So there won't be any doubt,
You're so wonderful to think of,
But so hard to be without

CB

I am the master of my fate,
I am the captain of my soul

William Ernest Henley

CB

Microcosm of Beauty *Robert Rendall*

I came to see the lofty mountain peaks:
It was the little things that held my gaze.
The alpine rose, the wild anemones,
And small green mountain lizards. Beetles too,
And butterflies competed with the view,
I could have watched these little things for weeks,
And smiled to see, contending for the eye.
A mountain challenged by a butterfly.

Look for me in Rainbows *Conn Bernard*

Time for me to go now, I won't say goodbye;
Look for me in rainbows, way up in the sky.
In the morning sunrise when all the world is new,
Just look for me and love me, as you know I loved you.

Time for me to leave you, I won't say goodbye;
Look for me in rainbows, high up in the sky.
In the evening sunset, when all the world is through,
Just look for me and love me, and I'll be close to you.

It won't be forever, the day will come and then
My loving arms will hold you, when we meet again.

Time for us to part now, we won't say goodbye;
Look for me in rainbows, shining in the sky.
Every waking moment, and all your whole life through
Just look for me and love me, as you know I loved you.

Just wish me to be near you,
And I'll be there with you.

☙

Fight One More Round *James Corbett*

When your feet are so tired that you have to shuffle back
to the centre of the ring, fight one more round.
When your arms are so tired that you can hardly lift your hands
to come on guard, fight one more round.
When your nose is bleeding and your eyes are black
and you are so tired you wish your opponent would crack
you one on the jaw and put you to sleep,
fight one more round – remembering that the man who always
fights one more round is never whipped.

The Swallow, the Owl, the Sandpiper and the Little Red Robin

The Knots Prayer *Anon*

Dear God:
Please untie the knots
that are in my mind,
my heart and my life.
Remove the have nots,
the can nots and the do nots
that I have in my mind.
Erase the will nots,
may nots,
might nots that may find
a home in my heart.
Release me from the could nots,
would nots and
should nots that obstruct my life.
And most of all,
Dear God,
I ask that you remove from my mind,
my heart and my life all of the 'am nots'
that I have allowed to hold me back,
especially the thought
that I am not good enough.
AMEN

⌘

ONE DAY
AT A TIME

Maddie's Magical Gift
Claire Barron

It is heartbreaking when a young person has a parent die. It doesn't seem right for anyone to not have a parent in their life when they grow up, graduate from school, get married and have children of their own. I have had the great fortune of working with children when they have either had a parent or a sibling die. I have facilitated many groups which provide children with an opportunity to see that others are experiencing something similar to help them feel less alone. As sad as these children are, they are also filled with great joy in these groups. People think there will be a lot of tears; there are always more laughs than tears. They bond, learn from one another and teach each other how to manage this terrible void in their lives. It provides them with a glimpse of normalcy.

Several years ago, I was leading a children's group for my local hospice. I was involved in the intake which allowed me to visit the children in their homes. I was able to meet their families and hear about the person who had died. I arrived at one house which happened to just be around the corner from where I live. I met Maddie, her mother and grandmother. We met at Maddie's grandmother's house; Maddie and her family lived about 20 minutes outside of town. Very quickly into our conversation, Maddie's mum took me aside and said, "I want to warn you, Maddie only wants to join this group if there is another girl her age whose father also died from a glioblastoma brain tumour." I told Maddie's mother that there was not someone in the group like that. What I didn't tell her is that in this particular group, Maddie was older than all the other children by 3 years.

In talking to Maddie, I discovered that her mum was right. Maddie was fixated on the idea that the only way for her to understand what had happened to her, would be if there was someone else her age who had experienced exactly the same thing she had experienced. In fact, she mentioned it three times in our ten minute chat. However, I did learn some things about her in between her plea to have someone like her in the group. Maddie was born

in Guelph, Ontario on September 13, 2006. She was ten when I met her. She loved to skate and do gymnastics. Her favourite thing about school was reading; she was a voracious reader. She had a grandmother with whom she spent a lot of time and she also had a dog she loved deeply. In the Summer, she liked to go camping. Maddie was a delightful girl, and I felt terrible knowing that the group would be starting the following week and there wasn't anyone in there with whom she could connect. Despite her reluctance, Maddie decided to join the group. "Maybe someone else will join," she said hopefully.

As I left the house, Maddie's grandmother talked to me and echoed what the others had said. "Maddie really needs to find someone who is going through the exact same thing as her. I know that it seems unrealistic but for some reason Maddie thinks that everything will be ok if she were to become friends someone with a shared experience. Someone who knows what it's like to have a dad with glioblastoma."

For the next couple of days I thought about Maddie. The program was about to start, and I knew that the person Maddie was looking for was not in the group. The day before the first session, we received a call from a mother. "I don't know why Leah is so interested in joining now, her dad died 2 years ago and we thought she was doing really well. She said that she doesn't feel sad but she just thought it would be fun to join this group."

Leah and her family also lived about 20 minutes out of town but in the opposite direction as Maddie. Leah was a bubbly, happy girl and very excited to meet me. She explained, "I don't know why I want to join this group. Of course, I still miss my dad but I am doing well. I thought I could make new friends though." This seemed promising to me as I asked her how old she was. When she said she was 10 I breathed a big sigh of relief. Finally there was someone

Maddie's age in this group. With trepidation, I asked how her dad died. "He had brain cancer – glioblastoma." I tried to contain my excitement. And for Leah's hobbies? She liked gymnastics, skating, reading and camping. She loved her dog and had a special connection with her grandmother. I kept turning back to Maddie's intake form to double check Maddie's answers. I couldn't believe it; they were almost identical.

At this point, my heart was racing not just because I was happy that Maddie's wish had come true but also because I felt like I was witnessing something so much bigger than a coincidence. I wanted to see how far this magic was going to go when I asked Leah what day she was born. Her answer overwhelmed me and I fought back tears. "September 13, 2006 at the hospital in Guelph." Maddie and Leah were born down the hall from one another. One was born in the morning and one was born in the evening.

I imagined Maddie's father and Leah's father holding their baby daughters at the hospital not knowing that they wouldn't live to see their girls grow up and not knowing that just down the hall would be the greatest support either of those girls could ever have.

Maddie and Leah met at the first session and hugged; they had been told of their similarities in advance. For the next eight weeks they sat together holding hands, finishing each other's sentences and acting like long lost sisters. Almost immediately, they made plans to get together outside of group. Maddie's world opened up. She had someone who had experienced exactly what she had and Leah was able to empathize and guide Maddie through her grief.

I used to see Maddie and Leah when they came to visit Maddie's grandmother. I would see them at a local Easter egg hunt together. More often than not, they were holding hands. They have remained friends bound by their common experience- just as Maddie predicted.

Sometimes beautiful magic happens after a loved one dies. It can be subtle or it can hit you like a ton of bricks. There are many explanations for when this happens but in Maddie and Leah's case, it would seem that their dads had something to do with this particular magic. Maddie asked for this connection to help her manage; it became Maddie's final and greatest gift from her dad.

The Owl

wisdom

൙

You will teach them to fly, but they will not fly your flight.
You will teach them to dream,
but they will not dream your dream.
You will teach them to live, but they will not live your life.
Nevertheless, in every flight, in every life, in every dream,
the print of the way you taught will always remain.

Mother Teresa

Legacy of Love *Anon*

A wife, a mother, a grandma too,
This is the legacy we have from you.
You taught us love and how to fight,
You gave us strength, you gave us might.
A stronger person would be hard to find,
And in your heart, you were always kind.
You fought for us all in one way or another,
Not just as a wife, not just as a mother.
For all of us you gave your best,
And now the time has come for you to rest.
So go in peace, you've earned your sleep,
Your love in our hearts, we'll eternally keep.

ೞ

When he shall die,

Take him and cut him out in little stars,

And he will make the face of heaven so fine

That all the world will be in love with night,

And pay no worship to the garish sun.

William Shakespeare, Scene 2, Romeo and Juliet wisdom

To live content with small means
William Henry Channing

To live content with small means; to seek elegance rather than luxury, and refinement rather than fashion, to be worthy, not respectable, and wealthy, not rich; to study hard, think quietly, talk gently, act frankly, to listen to stars and birds, to babes and sages, with open heart, to bear all cheerfully, to all bravely await occasions, hurry never. In a word, to let the spiritual unbidden and unconscious grow up through the common.
This is to be my symphony. Your love in our hearts, we'll eternally keep.

☙

CRYING DOES NOT INDICATE THAT YOU ARE WEAK. SINCE BIRTH, IT HAS ALWAYS BEEN A SIGN THAT YOU ARE ALIVE.

Charlotte Brontë, Jane Eyre

☙

If you're struggling, you deserve to make self-care a priority
Daniell Koepke

If you're struggling, you deserve to make self-care a priority. Whether that means lying in bed all day, eating comfort food, putting off homework, crying, sleeping, rescheduling plans, finding an escape through a good book, watching your favorite tv show, or doing nothing at all – give yourself permission to put your healing first. Quiet the voice telling you to do more and be more, and today, whatever you do, let it be enough. Feel your feelings, breathe, and be gentle with yourself. Acknowledge that you're doing the best you can to cope and survive. And trust that during this time of struggle, it's enough.

Poem of Life *Anon*

Life is but a stopping place,
A pause in what's to be,
A resting place along the road,
to sweet eternity.
We all have different journeys,
Different paths along the way,
We all were meant to learn some things,
but never meant to stay...

Our destination is a place,
Far greater than we know.
For some, the journey's quicker,
For some, the journey's slow.
And when the journey finally ends,
We'll claim a great reward,
And find an everlasting peace,
Together with the Lord.

cx

The world needs dreamers
and the world needs doers
But above all
The world
needs dreamers who do.

Sarah Ban Breathnach

I am Free *Anne Lindgren*

Don't grieve for me, for now I'm free, I'm following paths God made for me
I took his hand I heard him call
Then turned, and bid farewell to all
I could not stay another day
To laugh, to love, to sing, to play Tasks left undone must stay that way I found
my peace... at close of play
And if my parting left a void
Then fill it with remembered joy
A friendship shared, a laugh, a kiss Ah yes, these things I too will miss.
Be not burdened... deep with sorrow
I wish you sunshine of tomorrow
My life's been full I've savoured much Good friends, good times
A loved one's touch
Perhaps my time seemed all too brief Don't lengthen it now with grief
Lift up your hearts and share with me, God wants me now... He set me free.

☙

Life Well Lived *Anon*

A life well lived is a precious gift,
of hope and strength and grace,
from someone who has made our world
a brighter, better place.

It's filled with moments, sweet and sad
with smiles and sometimes tears,
with friendships formed and good times shared,
and laughter through the years.

A life well lived is a legacy,
of joy and pride and pleasure,
a living, lasting memory
our grateful heart's will treasure

The Owl

Many of my well-wishers often ask me *Anon*

Many of my well-wishers often ask me:
How old are you?
I tell them:
How can I answer this question?

When I play with a little child
I am one year old.

When I watch cartoons
I'm three.

When I dance to the tune of music, I am sweet sixteen.

And yes, when I try to heal someone's wound, I'm sure I've crossed six
decades of my life span.

And when I chat with sparrows or run after my dog and his ball,
I become their age.

What is there in age?
Isn't it a number only?
Like the light of the sun
And the flowing river waters
I am ageless.
I keep changing with time and the experience.

Days are marching towards night
No doubt,
Whenever it extends its hand
I shall hold it.

Till then It's not my age that matters.
How fully have I lived thus far,
That is the consideration.

Advice From A Tree *Ilan Shamir*

Dear Friend,
Stand Tall and Proud
Sink your roots deeply into the Earth
Reflect the light of a greater source
Think long term
Go out on a limb
Remember your place among all living beings
Embrace with joy the changing seasons
For each yields its own abundance
The Energy and Birth of Spring
The Growth and Contentment of Summer
The Wisdom to let go of leaves in the Fall
The Rest and Quiet Renewal of Winter
Feel the wind and the sun
And delight in their presence
Look up at the moon that shines down upon you
And the mystery of the stars at night.
Seek nourishment from the good things in life
Simple pleasures
Earth, fresh air, light
Be content with your natural beauty
Drink plenty of water
Let your limbs sway and dance in the breezes
Be flexible
Remember your roots
Enjoy the view!

CB

EVERY TIME YOU FIND SOME HUMOUR IN A DIFFICULT SITUATION, YOU WIN

This Being Human is a Guest House *Rumi*

This being human is a guest house.
Every morning a new arrival.
A joy, a depression, a meanness,
some momentary awareness comes
as an unexpected visitor.

Welcome and entertain them all!
Even if they're a crowd of sorrows,
who violently sweep your house
empty of its furniture,
still, treat each guest honourably.
He may be clearing you out
for some new delight.

The dark thought, the shame, the malice,
meet them at the door laughing,
and invite them in.
Be grateful for whoever comes,
because each has been sent
as a guide from beyond.

cx

DON'T TRY TO 'BE' HAPPY. HAPPINESS WILL FLOW FROM A LIFE OF SERVICE TO OTHERS.

Norman Wilson-Smith

All the darkness in the world
cannot extinguish the light of a single candle

St. Francis of Assisi

☙

Solitude Ella Wheeler Wilcox

Laugh, and the world laughs with you;
Weep, and you weep alone;
For the sad old earth must borrow its mirth,
But has trouble enough of its own.
Sing, and the hills will answer;
Sigh, it is lost on the air;
The echoes bound to a joyful sound,
But shrink from voicing care.

Rejoice, and men will seek you;
Grieve, and they turn and go;
They want full measure of all your pleasure,
But they do not need your woe.
Be glad, and your friends are many;
Be sad, and you lose them all, –
There are none to decline your nectared wine,
But alone you must drink life's gall.

Feast, and your halls are crowded;
Fast, and the world goes by.
Succeed and give, and it helps you live,
But no man can help you die.
There is room in the halls of pleasure
For a large and lordly train,
But one by one we must all file on
Through the narrow aisles of pain.

The Owl

10 Absolutes of Communicating through Alzheimer's

1.   Never argue, instead agree.
2.   Never reason, instead divert.
3.   Never shame, instead distract.
4.   Never lecture, reassure.
5.   Never say "remember", instead say reminisce.
6.   Never say "I told you", instead repeat/regroup.
7.   Never say you can't, instead do what they can.
8.   Never command/demand, instead ask/model.
9.   Never condescend, instead encourage/praise
10.   Never force, instead reinforce

☙

Never Trust a Mirror *Erin Hanson*

Never trust a mirror,
For the mirror always lies,
It makes you think that all your worth,
Can be seen from the outside.
Never trust a mirror,
It only shows you skin deep,
You can't see how your eyelids flutter,
When you're drifting off to sleep,
It doesn't show you what he sees,
When you're only being you,
Or how your eyes just light up,
When you're loving what you do,
It doesn't capture when you're smiling,
Where no one else can see,
And your reflection cannot tell you,
Everything you mean to me,
Never trust a mirror,
For it only shows your skin,
And if you think that it dictates your worth,
It's time you looked within.

If it comes; let it. If it goes; let it.

☙

Success is speaking words of praise *Anon*

Success is speaking words of praise,
In cheering other people's ways.
In doing just the best you can,
With every task and every plan.
It's silence when your speech would hurt,
Politeness when your neighbour's curt.
It's deafness when the scandal flows,
And sympathy with others' woes.
It's loyalty when duty calls,
It's courage when disaster falls.
It's patience when the hours are long,
It's found in laughter and in song.

Do Not Stand at My Grave and Weep _Clare Harner_

Do not stand at my grave and weep,
I am not there, I do not sleep.
I am a thousand winds that blow.
I am the diamond glint on snow.
I am the sunlight on ripened grain.
I am the gentle autumn rain.
When you wake in the morning hush,
I am the swift, uplifting rush
Of quiet birds in circling flight.
I am the soft starlight at night.
Do not stand at my grave and weep.
I am not there, I do not sleep.
(Do not stand at my grave and cry.
I am not there, I did not die!)

છ

May the blessing of light be on you _Scottish Blessing_

May the blessing of light be on you, light without and light within. May the blessed sunlight shine on you like a great peat fire, so that stranger and friend may come and warm himself at it. And may light shine out of the two eyes of you, like a candle set in the window of a house, bidding the wanderer come in out of the storm. And may the blessing of the rain be on you, may it beat upon your Spirit and wash it fair and clean, and leave there a shining pool where the blue of Heaven shines, and sometimes a star. And may the blessing of the earth be on you, soft under your feet as you pass along the roads, soft under you as you lie out on it, tired at the end of day; and may it rest easy over you when, at last, you lie out under it. May it rest so lightly over you that your soul may be out from under it quickly; up and off and on its way to God. And now may the Lord bless you, and bless you kindly.

When I'm Gone *Lyman Hancock*

When I come to the end of my journey
And I travel my last weary mile
Just forget if you can, that I ever frowned
And remember only the smile

> Forget unkind words I have spoken
> Remember some good I have done
> Forget that I ever had heartache
> And remember I've had loads of fun

Forget that I've stumbled and blundered
And sometimes fell by the way
Remember I have fought some hard battles
And won, ere the close of the day

> Then forget to grieve for my going
> I would not have you sad for a day
> But in summer just gather some flowers
> And remember the place where I lay

And come in the shade of evening
When the sun paints the sky in the west
Stand for a few moments beside me
And remember only my best.

℘

The young can be very lovely, but the faces of the old can be truly beautiful. Every line and fold, every contour and wrinkle of Sister Monica Joan's fine white skin revealed her character, strength, courage, humanity and irrepressible humour.

Jennifer Worth

The Owl

What Life Should Be *Pat A. Fleming*

To learn while still a child
What this life is meant to be.
To know it goes beyond myself,
It's so much more than me.

To overcome the tragedies,
To survive the hardest times.
To face those moments filled with pain,
And still manage to be kind.

To fight for those who can't themselves,
To always share my light.
With those who wander in the dark,
To love with all my might.

To still stand up with courage,
Though standing on my own.
To still get up and face each day,
Even when I feel alone.

To try to understand the ones
That no one cares to know.
And make them feel some value
When the world has let them go.

To be an anchor, strong and true,
That person loyal to the end.
To be a constant source of hope
To my family and my friends.

To live a life of decency,
To share my heart and soul.
To always say I'm sorry
When I've harmed both friend and foe.

To be proud of whom I've tried to be,
And this life I chose to live.
To make the most of every day
By giving all I have to give.

To me that's what this life should be,
To me that's what it's for.
To take what God has given me
And make it so much more

To live a life that matters,
To be someone of great worth.
To love and be loved in return
And make my mark on Earth.

∞

Our friends go with us as we go
Down the long path where
Beauty wends,
Where all we love forgathers, so
Why should we fear to join
our friends?

Oliver St. John Gogarty

The Owl

To Daffodils *Robert Herrick*

Fair daffodils, we weep to see
You haste away so soon:
As yet the early-rising sun
Has not attained his noon
Stay, stay
Until the hasting day
Has run
But to the evensong;
And having prayed together, we
Will go with you along.
We have short time to stay as you;
We have as short a spring;
As quick a growth to meet decay,
As you or anything.
We die,
As your hours do, and dry away
Like to the summers rain;
Or as the pearls of morning dew,
Ne'er to be found again.

ೞ

IF YOU HOLD SAND TOO TIGHTLY IN YOUR HAND IT WILL SLIP THROUGH YOUR FINGERS

Four-Leaf Clover *Ella Higginson*

I know a place where the sun is like gold,
    And the cherry blooms burst with snow,
And down underneath is the loveliest nook,
    Where the four-leaf clovers grow.

One leaf is for hope, and one is for faith,
    And one is for love, you know,
And God put another in for luck—
    If you search, you will find where they grow.

But you must have hope, and you must have faith,
    You must love and be strong - and so -
If you work, if you wait, you will find the place
    Where the four-leaf clovers grow.

ɔ

*We are such stuff as dreams are made on
And our little life is rounded with a sleep*

ɔ

Epitaph On A Friend *Robert Burns*

An honest man here lies at rest,
The friend of man, the friend of truth,
The friend of age, and guide of youth:
Few hearts like his, with virtue warm'd,
Few heads with knowledge so inform'd;
If there's another world, he lives in bliss;
If there is none, he made the best of this.

Death is Nothing at All...
Canon Henry Scott Holland

I have only slipped away into the next room.
I am I and you are you.
Whatever we were to each other that we are still.
Call me by my old familiar name.
Speak to me in the easy way which you always used.
Put no difference in your tone; wear no forced air of solemnity or sorrow.
Laugh as we always laughed at the little jokes we enjoyed together.
Play, smile, think of me, pray for me.
Let my name be ever the household word that it always was.
Let it be spoken without effort, without the ghost of a shadow on it.
Life means all that it ever meant.
It is the same as it ever was; there is absolutely unbroken continuity.
Why should I be out of mind because I am out of sight?
I am waiting for you for an interval,
somewhere very near, just around the corner.
All is well.

⍥

"You are beginning to understand, aren't you?
That the whole world is inside you –
in your perspectives and in your heart.
That to be able to find peace,
you must be at peace with yourself first;
and to truly enjoy life,
you must enjoy who you are.
Once you learn how to master this,
you will be protected from everything
that makes you feel like you cannot go on.
With this gift of recognising yourself,
even when you are alone,
you will never be lonely."

"As I walked out the door toward the gate that would lead to my freedom, I knew if I didn't leave my bitterness and hatred behind, I'd still be in prison."

Nelson Mandela

cx

This above all – to thine own self be true

Hamlet Act Sc 3

cx

There is No Night Without a Dawning
by Helen Steiner Rice

There is no night without a dawning,
No winter without a spring;
And beyond death's dark horizon
Our hearts, once more, will sing
For those who leave us for a while
have only 'gone away'
Out of a restless, careworn world
Into a brighter day.

The Owl

I Love to Sit in Silence *Anon*

I love to sit in silence
Beneath the shady trees
And listen to the song of birds
And to the buzz of bees.

I love to sit in silence
And watch the Clouds roll by
Then read a book or sing a song
And hear the wild bird cry.

I love to sit in silence
When the day is almost done
And see behind the distant hill
The paint glow of the sun.

I love to sit in silence
In the evening twilight
And listen to the nightjar
Singing with all its might.

I love to sit in silence
Beneath the Starry sky
And pray to all in earnest
To live in silence all the while.

cz

IN SHORT, THERE ARE
THREE THINGS THAT LAST;
FAITH, HOPE AND LOVE,
...THE GREATEST OF THESE IS LOVE

After becoming President...

After becoming President, I asked some of my bodyguard members to go for a walk in town. After the walk, we went for lunch at a restaurant. We sat in one of the most central ones, and each of us asked what we wanted. After a bit of waiting, the waiter who brought our menus appeared, at that moment I realised that at the table that was right in front of ours there was a single man waiting to be served.

When he was served, I told one of my soldiers: go ask that man to join us. The soldier went and transmitted my invitation. The man stood up, took the plate and sat next to me. While eating, his hands were constantly shaking and he didn't lift his head from the food. When we finished, he waved at me without even looking at me, I shook his hand and walked away!

Soldier said to me:
– Madiba, that man must be very sick as his hands wouldn't stop shaking while he was eating.
Not at all! The reason for his tremor is another – I replied. They looked at me weird and said to them:
– That man was the guardian of the jail I was locked up in. Often, after the torture I was subjected to, I screamed and cried for water and he came to humiliate me, he laughed at me and instead of giving me water he urinated on my head.

He wasn't sick, he was scared and shook maybe fearing that I, now that I'm president of South Africa, would send him to jail and do the same thing he did with me, torturing and humiliating him. But that's not me, that behaviour is not part of my character nor my ethics. Minds that seek revenge destroy states, while those that seek reconciliation build Nations.

Nelson Mandela

The Owl

I asked a friend who has crossed 70 and is heading towards 80 what sort of changes he is feeling in himself? He sent me this:

1 After loving my parents, my siblings, my spouse, my children and my friends, I have now started loving myself.

2 I have realised that I am not "Atlas". The world does not rest on my shoulders.

3 I have stopped bargaining with vegetable and fruit vendors. A few pennies more is not going to break me, but it might help the poor fellow save for his daughter's school fees.

4 I leave my waitress a big tip. The extra money might bring a smile to her face. She is toiling much harder for a living than I am.

5 I stopped telling the elderly that they've already narrated that story many times. The story makes them walk down memory lane and relive their past.

6 I have learned not to correct people even when I know they are wrong. The onus of making everyone perfect is not on me. Peace is more precious than perfection.

7 I give compliments freely and generously. Compliments are a mood enhancer not only for the recipient, but also for me. And a small tip for the recipient of a compliment, never, NEVER turn it down, just say "Thank You."

8 I have learned not to bother about a crease or a spot on my shirt. Personality speaks louder than appearances.

9 I walk away from people who don't value me. They might not know my worth, but I do.

10 I remain cool when someone plays dirty to outrun me in the rat race. I am not a rat and neither am I in any race.

11 I am learning not to be embarrassed by my emotions. It's my emotions that make me human.

12 I have learned that it's better to drop the ego than to break a relationship. My ego will keep me aloof, whereas with relationships, I will never be alone.

13 I have learned to live each day as if it's the last.
After all, it might be the last.

14 I am doing what makes me happy. I am responsible for my happiness, and I owe it to myself. Happiness is a choice. You can be happy at any time, just choose to be!

⋈

Life is supposed to be fun. It's not a job or occupation. We're here only once and we should have a bit of a laugh.

Billy Connolly

The Owl

To Be Present at the Time of Death
Jennifer Worth

To be present at the time of death can be one of the most important moments in life. To see those last, awesome minutes of transition from life into death can only be described as a spiritual experience. And then afterwards, when the body lies still, one gets the strange feeling that the person has simply gone away, as though he has said, 'I'm just going into the other room. I'll leave that thing there while I'm gone; I won't be needing it.' It's a very odd experience – the body is there, but the person has gone. No one would say, 'I am a body'; we say, 'I have a body'. So what, therefore, is the 'I'? The 'I' or perhaps 'me' has just stepped into the other room. It is a strange feeling, and I can't describe it in any other way. Another thing that is strange is that the body left behind looks smaller, quite a lot smaller, than the living person. The face looks the same, but calm and relaxed, wrinkles and worry lines are smoothed, and a feeling of serenity pervades the entire room. But the person, the 'I', has gone. It also greatly helps the process of mourning to see the body after death, and preferably to assist in the laying out. Nurses used to do the job when I was young girl, and we always asked the relatives if they wanted to help. Nurses don't do it anymore, but anyone can ask.

☙

Everybody needs beauty, as well as bread; places to play in and places to pray in, where nature may heal and give strength to body and soul

John Muir

108

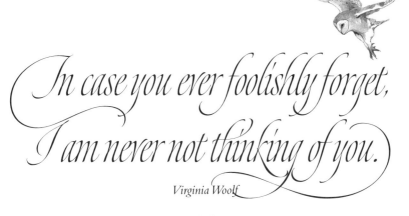

In case you ever foolishly forget,
I am never not thinking of you.

Virginia Woolf

☙

A Silent Tear
Anon

Just close your eyes and you will see
All the memories that you have of me
Just sit and relax and you will find
I'm really still there inside your mind
Don't cry for me now I'm gone
For I am in the land of song
There is no pain, there is no fear
So dry away that silent tear
Don't think of me in the dark and cold
For here I am, no longer old
I'm in that place that's filled with love
Known to you all, as 'up above'

☙

THE HEART OF MAN IS VERY MUCH
LIKE THE SEA, IT HAS ITS STORMS,
IT HAS ITS TIDES AND IN ITS DEPTHS
IT HAS ITS PEARLS TOO

Vincent van Gogh

The Owl

Letter from a Mother to a Daughter
Guillermo Gómez-Peña

My dear girl, the day you see I'm getting old, I ask you to please be patient, but most of all, try to understand what I'm going through.

If when we talk, I repeat the same thing a thousand times, don't interrupt to say: 'You said the same thing a minute ago'… Just listen, please. Try to remember the times when you were little and I would read the same story night after night until you would fall asleep.

When I don't want to take a bath, don't be mad and don't embarrass me. Remember when I had to run after you making excuses and trying to get you to take a shower when you were just a girl?

When you see how ignorant I am when it comes to new technology, give me the time to learn and don't look at me that way… remember, honey, I patiently taught you how to do many things like eating appropriately, getting dressed, combing your hair and dealing with life's issues every day… the day you see I'm getting old, I ask you to please be patient, but most of all, try to understand what I'm going through.

If I occasionally lose track of what we're talking about, give me the time to remember, and if I can't, don't be nervous, impatient or arrogant. Just know in your heart that the most important thing for me is to be with you.

And when my old, tired legs don't let me move as quickly as before, give me your hand the same way that I offered mine to you when you first walked.

When those days come, don't feel sad… just be with me, and understand me while I get to the end of my life with love.

I'll cherish and thank you for the gift of time and joy we shared. With a big smile and the huge love I've always had for you, I just want to say, I love you… my darling daughter.

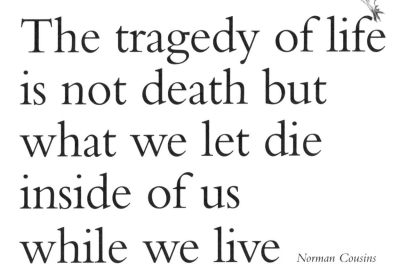

The tragedy of life is not death but what we let die inside of us while we live

Norman Cousins

☙

I Am
Anon

I am the wind in the trees
and the song of a bird.
I am moonbeams in a midnight sky
and a glorious rainbow after the storm.
I am morning dew
and freshly-fallen snow.
I am a butterfly flying overhead
and a puppy happily at play.
I am a gentle touch
a warm embrace.
Open your heart to know...I am not gone.
Reach deep into your soul...You will find me.
I am here.
Have no fear, I am with you,
Always.

Be Grateful for Freedom
Ben Okri

Be grateful for freedom
To see other dreams.
Bless your loneliness as much as you drank
Of your former companionships.
All that you are experiencing now
Will become moods of future joys
So bless it all.
Do not think your ways superior
To another's
Do not venture to judge
But see things with fresh and open eyes
Do not condemn
But praise what you can
And when you can't be silent.

Time is now a gift for you
A gift of freedom
To think and remember and understand
The ever perplexing past
And to re-create yourself anew
In order to transform time.

Live while you are alive.
Learn the ways of silence and wisdom
Learn to act, learn a new speech
Learn to be what you are in the seed of your spirit
Learn to free yourself from all things that have moulded you
And which limit your secret and undiscovered road.

Remember that all things which happen
To you are raw materials
Endlessly fertile
Endlessly yielding of thoughts that could change

Your life and go on doing forever.

Never forget to pray and be thankful
For all the things good or bad on the rich road;
For everything is changeable
So long as you live while you are alive.

Fear not, but be full of light and love;
Fear not but be alert and receptive;
Fear not but act decisively when you should;
Fear not, but know when to stop;
Fear not for you are loved by me;
Fear not, for death is not the real terror,
But life -magically – is.

Be joyful in your silence
Be strong in your patience
Do not try to wrestle with the universe
But be sometimes like water or air
Sometimes like fire

Live slowly, think slowly, for time is a mystery.
Never forget that love
Requires that you be
The greatest person you are capable of being,
Self-generating and strong and gentle-
Your own hero and star.

Love demands the best in us
To always and in time overcome the worst
And lowest in our souls.
Love the world wisely.

The Owl

It is love alone that is the greatest weapon
And the deepest and hardest secret.

So fear not, my friend.
The darkness is gentler than you think.
Be grateful for the manifold
Dreams of creation
And the many ways of unnumbered peoples.

Be grateful for life as you live it.
And may a wonderful light

☙

The day you walk in another's shoes is
the day you understand their journey.
Until then don't assume you know
anything about how they feel and
survive what they have been given
to bear. Be careful for what you lack
compassion for because life has a way
of sending you what you fail to show
a caring heart towards.

Darla Evans

Watch, O Lord...
St Augustine

Watch, O Lord, with those who wake, or watch, or weep tonight,
and give Your angels and saints charge over those who sleep.
Tend Your sick ones, O Lord Christ.
Rest Your weary ones.
Bless Your dying ones.
Soothe Your suffering ones.
Pity Your afflicted ones.
Shield Your joyous ones, and all for Your love's sake.
AMEN.

⅌

THE TRAIN: *Anon*

At birth we boarded the train and met our parents, and we believe
they will always travel by our side. As time goes by, other people
will board the train; and they will be significant i.e. our siblings,
friends, children, strangers and even the love of your life. However,
at some station our parents will step down from the train, leaving
us on this journey alone. Others will step down over time and leave
a permanent vacuum. Some, however, will go so unnoticed that we
don't realise they vacated their seats. This train ride will be full of joy,
sorrow, fantasy, expectations, hellos, goodbyes, and farewells. Success
consists of having a good relationship with all passengers requiring
that we give the best of ourselves.
The mystery to everyone is: We do not know at which station we
ourselves will step down. So, we must live in the best way, love,
forgive, and offer the best of who we are. It is important to do this
because when the time comes for us to step down and leave our seat
empty we should leave behind beautiful memories for those who will
continue to travel on the train of life.
I wish you a joyful journey for the coming years on your train of
life. Reap success, give lots of love and be happy. More importantly,
thank God for the journey!

The Owl

When I Am Dead, My Dearest
Christina Rossetti

When I am dead, my dearest,
Sing no sad songs for me;
Plant thou no roses at my head,
Nor shady cypress-tree:
Be the green grass above me
With showers and dewdrops wet;
And if thou wilt, remember,
And if thou wilt, forget.

I shall not see the shadows,
I shall not feel the rain;
I shall not hear the nightingale
Sing on, as if in pain:
And dreaming through the twilight
That doth not rise nor set,
Haply I may remember,
And haply may forget.

ᘓ

❝

Life is funny isn't it? Just when you think you've got
it all figured out, just when you finally begin to plan
something, get excited about something, and feel
like you know what direction you're heading in, the
paths change, the signs change, the wind blows the
other way, north is suddenly south, and east is west,
and you're lost. It is so easy to lose your way, to lose
direction. And that's with following all the signposts

Cecelia Ahern ❞

116

Feel No Guilt in Laughter *Anon*

Feel no guilt in laughter, he'd know how much you care.
Feel no sorrow in a smile that he is not here to share.
You cannot grieve forever; he would not want you to.
He'd hope that you could live your life the way you always do.
So, talk about the good times and the way you showed you cared,
the days you spent together, all the happiness you shared.
Let memories surround you, a word someone may say
will suddenly recapture a time, an hour or a day,
that brings him back as clearly as though he were still here,
and fills you with the feeling that he is always near.
For if you keep those moments, you will never be apart
and he will live forever locked safely within your heart.

☙

It is Well-nigh Impossible to Talk to Anyone about Death

"It is well-nigh impossible to talk to anyone about death, I find. Most
people seem deeply embarrassed. It is like when I was a girl and nobody
could talk about sex. We all did it, but nobody talked about it! We have
now grown out of that silly taboo, and we must grow out of our inhibitions
surrounding death. They have arisen largely because so few people see
death any more, even though it is quite obviously in our midst. A cultural
change must come, a new atmosphere of freedom, which will only happen
if we open our closed minds."

Jennifer Worth

☙

The shell must be broken before the bird can fly

Kindness is my Number One Attribute in a Human Being

"I think probably kindness is my number one attribute in a human being. I'll put it before any of the things like courage or bravery or generosity or anything else."

Brian Sibley: **or brains even?**

"Oh gosh, yes, brains is one of the least. You can be a lovely person without brains, absolutely lovely. Kindness – that simple word. To be kind – it covers everything, to my mind. If you're kind that's it."

Roald Dahl

෫ඁ

WHERE FLOWERS BLOOM SO DOES HOPE

Lady Bird Johnson

෫ඁ

Do You Pray?

"What's a prayer? Prayer doesn't only happen when we kneel or clasp our hands together and focus upon and expect things from God. Thinking positive and wishing good for others is a prayer. When you hug a friend, that's a prayer. When you cook something to nourish family and friends, that's a prayer. When we send off our near and dear ones and say, 'drive safely', or 'be safe', that's a prayer. When you're helping someone in need by giving your time and energy, you're praying. When you forgive someone, that's a prayer. Prayer is a vibration. A feeling. A thought. Prayer is the voice of love, friendship, genuine relationships. Prayer is an expression of your silent being. Keep praying always..."

Anon

Let yourself be silently drawn
by the strange pull of what you really love.
It will not lead you astray

Rumi

ᘓ

Go to That Place we Loved
Anon

Go to that place we loved, our secret place,
Close your eyes and you'll see my face.
Play that tune, the tune we loved to hear,
Close your eyes and you'll see me clear.
Walk on the beach or climb to the top of a hill,
Close your eyes and you'll see me still.
Take a sip of wine, of dark red wine,
Close your eyes and you'll see me fine.
At night go out and look at the brightest star,
Close your eyes and you'll see me far.
On a day when the sky is blue and cold and clear
Close your eyes and you'll see me near.
Take down a book that would have been my choice,
Open the book, close your eyes.
You'll hear my voice.

ᘓ

IT IS SO. IT CANNOT BE OTHERWISE

Inscription on the Ruins of a 15th Century Cathedral in Amsterdam

We can all Endure
Mark Beaumont

Young or old, female or male, we can all go further.
'The origin of the words 'Endure' is 15th century old French,
from Endurer 'to make hard.' The ability to withstand wear
and tear of a difficult situation.

The Scandinavians have a phrase, 'the doorstep mile,' meaning
that the first mile away from your front door is the hardest of
all. This might be a physical journey but in the metaphoric
sense the doorstep mile is your ability to take the first step
and commit. Something you could easily daydream about
but never action. I am a big fan of dreams but they mean
little without the belief system and habit of turning them into
realities. We are creatures of habit so therefore committing
to ideas is a habit. People who enjoy lots of adventures in
life have formed a habit rather than letting them fizzle away
to forgotten wish lists. The scale of any new journey can be
intimidating but before any of that you must commit to the
dream. So here is the trick, be brave for 20 seconds. This is
long enough to tell your friend, it is a lot harder to not do
something when you have told someone you respect that you
will do it. This is what I tell my children every time they do
something new. Jenny Graham, the female Round the World
record holder from Inverness, found it difficult to tell people
she planned to cycle around the world, she just wasn't sure
she was 'that' person. But saying it out loud to people you
trust is an empowering step. After that you get caught up in
the excitement of doing rather than the procrastination of
thinking. In the context of being an endurance bike rider, this
could mean leaving the comfort of your local loops or daily
commute when you want to test your character: physically,
mentally, socially and psychologically. You know you are an
endurance bike rider when you don't just crave cafe bike
culture, you crave freedom.

NOTHING BINDS PEOPLE MORE STRONGLY
THAN THE SAME SENSE OF HUMOUR,
AND THE ABILITY TO LAUGH TOGETHER.

Jennifer Worth

ॐ

More Than Anything Else, a Dying Person Needs...

"More than anything else, a dying person needs to have someone with them. This used to be recognised in hospitals, and when I trained, no one ever died alone. However busy the wards, or however short the staff, a nurse was always assigned to sit with a dying person to hold their hand, stroke their forehead, or whisper a few words. Peace and quietness, even reverence for the dying, were expected and assured.

I disagree wholly with the notion that there is no point in staying with an unconscious patient because he or she does not know you are there. I am perfectly certain, though years of experience and observation, that unconsciousness, as we define it, is not a state of knowing. Rather, it is a state of knowing and understanding on a different level that is beyond our immediate experience."

Jennifer Worth

ॐ

*The tree which moves some to tears of joy
is in the eyes of others only a green thing
that stands in the way*

William Blake

After I Have Gone
Vera Arlett

Speak my name softly after I have gone.
I loved the quiet things, the flowers and the dew,
Field mice; birds homing; and the frost that shone
On nursery windows when my years were few;
And autumn mists subduing hill and plain
and blurring outlines of those older moods
that follow, after loss and grief and pain
And last and best, a gentle laugh with friends,
All bitterness foregone, and evening near.
If we be kind and faithful when day ends,
We shall not meet that ragged starveling 'fear'
As one by one we take the unknown way
Speak my name softly – there's no more to say

℃ℨ

Everyone deserves a chance to fly!

Stephen Schwartz

℃ℨ

My Father's house has many rooms; if that
were not so, would I have told you that I am
going there to prepare a place for you? And if
I go and prepare a place for you, I will come
back and take you to be with me that you also
may be where I am. You know the way to the
place where I am going.

John 14.2-3

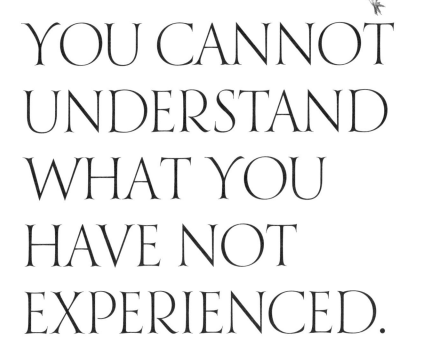

YOU CANNOT UNDERSTAND WHAT YOU HAVE NOT EXPERIENCED.

Jennifer Worth

○3

Be comfortable with uncertainty
Sandy Rough

Be comfortable with uncertainty
and life sometimes gets interesting
with things we wouldn't otherwise have expected.

Clamour for certainty,
and there is a more than fair chance
that we will be disappointed.

I had Spent an Hour in the Bank
Vera Arlett

I had spent an hour in the bank with my dad, as he had to transfer some money. I couldn't resist myself and asked...

"Dad, why don't we activate your internet banking?"
"Why would I do that?" He asked...
"Well, then you won't have to spend an hour here for things like transfer. You can even do your shopping online. Everything will be so easy!"
I was so excited about initiating him into the world of Net banking.
He asked "If I do that, I won't have to step out of the house?
"Yes, yes"! I said. I told him how even grocery can be delivered at door now and how amazon delivers everything!

His answer left me tongue-tied.

He said "Since I entered this bank today, I have met four of my friends, I have chatted a while with the staff who know me very well by now.
You know I am alone... this is the company that I need. I like to get ready and come to the bank. I have enough time, it is the physical touch that I crave.
Two years back I got sick, The store owner from whom I buy fruits, came to see me and sat by my bedside and cried.
When your Mum fell down few days back while on her morning walk.
Our local grocer saw her and immediately got his car to rush her home as he knows where I live.
Would I have that 'human' touch if everything became online?
Why would I want everything delivered to me and force me to interact with just my computer?
I like to know the person that I'm dealing with and not just the 'seller'. It creates bonds of relationships.

Does Amazon deliver all this as well?"'

Technology isn't life... Spend time with people .. Not with devices."

Create whatever causes a revolution in your heart.
The rest will take care of itself

Elizabeth Gilbert

❧

For Equilibrium, a Blessing:
John O'Donohue

Like the joy of the sea coming home to shore,
May the relief of laughter rinse through your soul.

As the wind loves to call things to dance,
May your gravity by lightened by grace.

Like the dignity of moonlight restoring the earth,
May your thoughts incline with reverence and respect.

As water takes whatever shape it is in,
So free may you be about who you become.

As silence smiles on the other side of what's said,
May your sense of irony bring perspective.

As time remains free of all that it frames,
May your mind stay clear of all it names.

May your prayer of listening deepen enough
to hear in the depths the laughter of god.

You build on failure
Johnny Cash

You build on failure.
You use it as a stepping stone.
Close the door on the past.
You don't try to forget the mistakes,
but you don't dwell on it.
You don't let it have any of your energy,
or any of your time,
or any of your space.

CB

*What good is the warmth of summer,
without the cold of winter to give it sweetness*
Travels with Charley: In Search of America

CB

"Believe there is a great power silently working all things for good. Behave yourself and never mind the rest" *Beatrix Potter*

CB

**Worry never robs tomorrow of its sorrow.
It only saps today of its joy.** *Leo Buscaglia*

CB

Regardless of how much or how little money you may have, it is a subject best talked about only selectively. Be a good listener, it will help you to develop an enquiring mind. I think that one has to be ready to start all over again any number of times.
                                                                      Abbot Herbert Byrne

Watch your thoughts
for they become words
Watch your words
for they become actions
Watch your actions
for they become habits
Watch your habits
for they become your character
And watch your character
for it becomes your destiny
What we think, we become

Lao Tzu

The Owl

“ I regret the passing of what I regard of as one of the great luxuries of civilisation – that is **solitude.** I think those snatched moments; the twenty minutes when you're waiting at the luggage carousel – you used to have to do nothing but go into your thoughts – now we all take out our phone because we've been deprived of a signal for a couple of hours in an aeroplane. Maybe we don't have quite a rich an inner life as we used to. But if you get into the habit of **solitude** (which is an entirely different thing from loneliness) – treat your mind as a garden that you can walk around in. It's generally a place to find more happiness. **”** *Ian McEwan*

HAPPY THE MAN WHO, DYING, CAN PLACE HIS HAND ON HIS HEART AND SAY: 'AT LEAST I DIDN'T NEGLECT TO TELL THE THRUSH HOW BEAUTIFULLY SHE SINGS

Bernard O'Donoghue

☙

We're All in the Queue

We're all in "the queue" without knowing it.
We will never know how many people are ahead of us.
We can't move to the bottom of the row.
We can't get out of line.
We can't avoid the queue.
So while we wait in line.
Make the moments count!
Make priorities.
Make the time.
Let your qualities be known.
Make people feel important.
Make your voice heard.
Make big things out of small things.
Make someone smile.
Make the change.
Make love.
Make Peace.
Make sure you tell your people you love them.
Make sure you have no regrets.
Make sure you're ready.

An African Elegy
Ben Okri

We are the miracles that God made
To taste the bitter fruit of Time.
We are precious.
And one day our suffering
Will turn into the wonders of the earth.

> There are things that burn me now
> Which turn golden when I am happy.
> Do you see the mystery of our pain?
> That we bear poverty
> And are able to sing and dream sweet things

And that we never curse the air when it is warm
Or the fruit when it tastes so good
Or the lights that bounce gently on the waters?
We bless things even in our pain.
We bless them in silence.

> That is why our music is so sweet.
> It makes the air remember.
> There are secret miracles at work
> That only Time will bring forth.
> I too have heard the dead singing.

And they tell me that
This life is good
They tell me to live it gently
With fire, and always with hope.
There is wonder here

> And there is surprise
> In everything the unseen moves.
> The ocean is full of songs.
> The sky is not an enemy.
> Destiny is our friend.

Tell us of Pain
Kahlil Gibran

And a woman spoke, saying, Tell us of Pain.
And he said:
Your pain is the breaking of the shell that encloses your understanding.
Even as the stone of the fruit must break, that its heart may stand in the
sun, so must you know pain.
And could you keep your heart in wonder at the daily miracles of your
life your pain would not seem less wondrous than your joy;
And you would accept the seasons of your heart, even as you have always
accepted the seasons that pass over your fields.
And you would watch with serenity through the winters of your grief.
Much of your pain is self-chosen.
It is the bitter potion by which the physician within you heals
your sick self.
Therefore trust the physician, and drink his remedy in silence
and tranquility:
For his hand, though heavy and hard, is guided by the tender hand
of the Unseen,
And the cup he brings, though it burn your lips, has been fashioned of
the clay which the Potter has moistened with His own sacred tears.

⁜

We can complain because rose bushes have thorns, or rejoice because thorn bushes have roses.

Abraham Lincoln

One of the Deepest Needs

Peter G van Breemen

One of the deepest needs of the human heart is the need to be appreciated.
Every human being wants to be valued… Every human being craves
to be accepted, accepted for what he is… When I am not accepted,
then something in me is broken… Acceptance means that the people
with whom I live give me a feeling of self-respect, a feeling that I am
worthwhile. They are happy that I am who I am. Acceptance means that I
am welcome to be myself. Acceptance means that though there is need for
growth, I am not forced. I do not have to be the person I am not!

ᘒ

Thoughts in Solitude

Thomas Merton

Things worth remembering:
The value of time,
The success of perseverance
The pleasure of working
The dignity of simplicity
The worth of character
The improvement of talent
The influence of example
The virtue of patience
The joy of originating
The power of kindness

ᘒ

Sadness is but a wall between two gardens

"DEATH IS SOMETHING INEVITABLE WHEN A MAN HAS DONE WHAT HE CONSIDERS TO BE HIS DUTY TO HIS PEOPLE AND HIS COUNTRY, HE CAN REST IN PEACE. I BELIEVE I HAVE MADE THAT EFFORT AND THAT IS, THEREFORE, WHY I WILL SLEEP FOR THE ETERNITY." *Nelson Mandela 1996*

Now the Day is Over
Anon

Now the day is over,
Night is drawing nigh,
Shadows of the evening
Steal across the sky.

Now the darkness gathers,
Stars begin to peep,
Birds, and beasts and flowers
Soon will be asleep.
Jesus, give the weary
Calm and sweet repose;
With Thy tenderest blessing
May mine eyelids close.

Grant to little children
Visions bright of Thee;
Guard the sailors tossing
On the deep, blue sea.
Comfort those who suffer,
Watching late in pain;
Those who plan some evil
From their sin restrain.

Through the long night watches
May Thine angels spread
Their white wings above me,
Watching round my bed.

CB

Kindnesses, like grain, grow by sowing

The Tide Rises, the Tide Falls
Henry Wadsworth Longfellow

The tide rises, the tide falls,
The twilight darkens, the curlew calls;
Along the sea-sands damp and brown
The traveller hastens toward the town,
    And the tide rises, the tide falls.

Darkness settles on roofs and walls,
But the sea, the sea in the darkness calls;
The little waves, with their soft, white hands,
Efface the footprints in the sands,
    And the tide rises, the tide falls.

The morning breaks; the steeds in their stalls
Stamp and neigh, as the hostler calls;
The day returns, but nevermore
Returns the traveller to the shore,
    And the tide rises, the tide falls.

☙

Let us not take ourselves too seriously.
None of us has a monopoly on wisdom,
and we must always be ready to listen
and respect other points of view

Queen Elizabeth II

Beautiful Things
Lucile Ballard

As we hurry along on life's journey today
With the joy and the sorrow it brings,
And never a thought what we pass on the way
Let us look for the beautiful things.

There is music that's free, that will surely beguile
'Tis the song of the bird as he sings,
And the sun-kissed breeze makes us linger awhile.
Just to look for the beautiful things.

Let us close our eyes to the faults of a friend
Drop them deep in oblivion's springs,
As we travel along to life's golden end
We can always find beautiful things.

☙

Don't judge each day
by the harvest you reap
but by the seeds that you plant

Robert Louis Stevenson

☙

NO ONE IS USELESS IN THIS WORLD WHO LIGHTENS THE BURDENS OF ANOTHER

Charles Dickens

"For what it's worth: it's never too late or, in my case, too early to be whoever you want to be. There's no time limit, stop whenever you want. You can change or stay the same, there are no rules to this thing. We can make the best or the worst of it." *Francis Scott Fitzgerald*

ೞ

Are You Happy?
Bianca Sparacino

"Are you happy?" "In all honesty? No. But I am curious
– I am curious in my sadness, and I am curious in my joy.
I am ever seeking, ever feeling. I am in awe of the beautiful
moments life gives us, and I am in awe of the difficult ones.
I am transfixed by grief, by growth. It is all so stunning, so
rich, and I will never convince myself that I cannot be somber,
cannot be hurt, cannot be overjoyed. I want to feel it all
– I don't want to cover it up or numb it. So no, I am not
happy. I am open, and I wouldn't have it any other way."

'It was my Teacher's Genius...'
Helen Kellor

"It was my teacher's genius, her quick sympathy, her loving tact because she seized the right moment to impart knowledge that made it so pleasant and acceptable to me. She realised that a child's mind is like a shallow brook which ripples and dances merrily over the stony course of its education and reflects here a flower, there a bush, yonder a fleecy cloud; and she attempted to guide my mind on its way, knowing that like a brook it should be fed by mountain streams and hidden springs, until it broadened out into a deep river, capable of reflecting in its placid surface, billowy hills, the luminous shadows of trees and the blue heavens, as well as the sweet face of a little flower. Any teacher can take a child to the classroom, but not every teacher can make him learn. He will not work joyously unless he feels that liberty is his, whether he is busy or at rest; he must feel the flush of victory and the heart-sinking of disappointment before he takes with a will the tasks distasteful to him and resolves to dance his way bravely through a dull routine of textbooks.

My teacher is so near to me that I scarcely think of myself apart from her. How much of my delight in all beautiful things is innate, and how much is due to her influence, I can never tell. I feel that her being is inseparable from my own, and that the footsteps of my life are in hers. All the best of me belongs to her – there is not a talent, or an aspiration or a joy in me that has not been awakened by her loving touch."

I'm Sending a Dove to Heaven
Anon

I'm sending a dove to Heaven
with a parcel on its wings
be careful when you open it
it's full of beautiful things

Inside are a million kisses
wrapped up in a million hugs
to say how much I miss you
and to send you all my love

I hold you close within my heart
and there you will remain
to walk with me throughout my life
until me meet again.

☙

You cannot hope to build a better world without improving the individuals. To that end each of us must work for his own improvement, and at the same time share a general responsibility for all humanity, our particular duty being to aid those to whom we think we can be most useful.

Marie Curie

My Mum Did Not Sleep
Anon

My mum did not sleep. She felt exhausted. She was irritable, grumpy, and bitter. She never felt well until one day, suddenly, she changed.

One day my dad said to her:
– I've been looking for a job for three months and I haven't found anything, I'm going to have a few beers with friends.
My mum replied:
– It's okay.
My brother said to her:
– Mum, I'm doing poorly in all subjects at the University.
My mum replied:
– Okay, you will recover, and if you don't, well, you repeat the year, but you pay the tuition.
My sister said to her:
– Mum, I crashed the car.
My mum replied:
– Okay daughter, take it to the car shop and find how to pay and while they fix it, get around by bus or subway.
Her daughter-in-law said to her:
– Mother-in-law, I came to spend a few months with you.
My mum replied:
– Okay, settle in the living room couch and look for some blankets in the closet.
All of us gathered worried to see these reactions coming from Mum.

We suspected that she had gone to the doctor and that she was prescribed some pills called "I don't give a damn"... Perhaps she was overdosing on these!

We then proposed to do an "intervention" to remove her from any possible addiction she had towards some anti-tantrum medication.

But then ... she gathered us around her and my mum explained:
"It took me a long time to realise that each person is responsible for
their life. It took me years to discover that my anguish, anxiety, my
depression, my courage, my insomnia and my stress, does not solve your
problems but aggravates mine.

I am not responsible for the actions of anyone and it's not my job to
provide happiness but I am responsible for the reactions I express to
that.

Therefore, I came to the conclusion that my duty to myself is to
remain calm and let each one of you solve what corresponds to you.

I have taken courses in yoga, meditation, miracles, human development,
mental hygiene, vibration and neurolinguistic programming and in all
of them, I found a common denominator in them all...

I can only control myself, you have all the necessary resources to solve
your own problems despite how hard they may be. My job is to pray
for you, love on you, encourage you but it's up to YOU to solve them
and find your happiness.

I can only give you my advice if you ask me and it depends on you to
follow it or not. There are consequences, good or bad, to your decisions
and YOU have to live them.

So from now on, I cease to be the receptacle of your responsibilities,
the sack of your guilt, the laundress of your remorse, the advocate of
your faults, the wall of your lamentations, the depositary of your duties,
who should solve your problems or spare a tire every time to fulfill
your responsibilities.

From now on, I declare all independent and self-sufficient adults.

Another Leaf has Fallen
Anon

Another leaf has fallen, another soul has gone.
But still we have God's promises,
in every robin's song.
For he is in His heaven,
and though He takes away,
He always leaves to mortals,
the bright sun's kindly ray.
He leaves the fragrant blossoms,
and lovely forest, green.
And gives us new found comfort,
when we on Him will lean.

cx

I have noticed that even those who assert that everything is predestined and that we can change nothing about it still look both ways before they cross the street.

Stephen Hawkins

cx

When we Love Deeply
Dr. Joanne Cacciatore

When we love deeply, we mourn deeply; extraordinary grief is an expression of extraordinary love. Grief and love mirror each other; one is not possible without the other. And Eternity in an hour.

Auguries of Innocence
William Blake

To see a World in a Grain of Sand
And a Heaven in a Wild Flower,
Hold Infinity in the palm of your hand
And Eternity in an hour.

☙

LISTEN TO YOUR PATIENT, HE IS TELLING YOU THE DIAGNOSIS

☙

Prayer for those who have died
Anon

Dying is the final healing
The last great adventure
It cannot be avoided
It is a harvest that we are
all working towards.
We need to learn the skills
of letting go long before
We come to our own completion
And know that death is not failure
But celebration after a life well-lived
However short or long that life might be.

☙

The Owl

"A few minutes ago every tree was excited, bowing to the roaring storm, waving, swirling, tossing their branches in glorious enthusiasm like worship. But though to the outer ear these trees are now silent, their songs never cease. Every hidden cell is throbbing with music and life, every fiber thrilling like harp strings, while incense is ever flowing from the balsam bells and leaves. No wonder the hills and groves were God's first temples, and the more they are cut down and hewn into cathedrals and churches, the farther off and dimmer seems the Lord himself."   *John Muir*

cs

OUR CHARACTERS ARE SHAPED BY OUR COMPANIONS AND BY THE OBJECTS TO WHICH WE GIVE MOST OF OUR THOUGHTS AND WITH WHICH WE FILL OUR IMAGINATIONS   *William Temple*

cs

The Greatest Gift
William Barclay, The Gospel of John

The greatest gift that any human being can give to another is the gift of understanding and of peace. To have someone to whom we can go to at any time, and know that they will not laugh at our dreams, or misunderstand our confidences is a most wonderful thing. It is open to all of us to make our own homes like that. This is something which does not cost money, and which does not need lavish and costly hospitality. It costs only the understanding heart.

144

Leadership is not about being the best.
Leadership is about making everyone else better

cx

The Men Whom I Have Seen Succeed
by Charles Kingsley

The men whom I have seen succeed best in life always have been cheerful and hopeful; who went about their business with a smile on their faces; and took the changes and chances of this mortal life like men; facing rough and smooth alike as it came., and so found the truth of the old proverb 'that good times and bad times and all times pass over'

cx

To be a strong hand in the dark to another in the time of need. *Hugh Black*

So Trustful are the Doves
Richard Jefferies

"So trustful are the doves, the squirrels, the birds of the branches, and the creatures of the field. Under their tuition let us rid ourselves of mental terrors, and face death itself as calmly as they do the livid lightning; so trustful and so content with their fate, resting in themselves and unappalled. If but by reason and will I could reach the godlike calm and courage of what we so thoughtlessly call the timid turtle-dove, I should lead a nearly perfect life."

☙

The ideals which have lighted my way, and time – after – time have given me new courage to face life cheerfully, have been kindness, beauty, and truth

Albert Einstein (1879-1955)

☙

The man who started life as a refugee prince ended it taken into the heart of his adopted country. For someone so no-nonsense there can be no more fitting epitaph than his own words. "Life's going to go on after me," he said. "If I can make life marginally more tolerable for the people who come after I'd be delighted."

Prince Philip

Wrinkles should merely indicate where smiles have been

Mark Twain

Jesus, Friend of all the Children
Anon

Jesus, Friend of all the children,
be my friend and guide.
Take my hand and ever keep me
at Your side.
Teach me how to grow in goodness
daily as I grow;
You have been a child, and surely
You will know.
Never leave me or forsake me,
ever be my friend;
for I need You from life's dawning
to its end.

ↀ

If you go looking for a friend, you're going to find they're very scarce. If you go out to be a friend, you'll find them everywhere.

ↀ

**Good night. Parting is such sweet sorrow,
that I shall say good night, till it be morrow.** *Romeo and Juliet*

Today we have no time even to look at each other
Mother Teresa

Today we have no time even to look at each other, to talk to each other, to enjoy each other, and still less to be what our children expect from us, what the husband expects from this wife, what the wife expects of her husband. And so less and less we are in touch with each other. The world is lost for want of sweetness and kindness. People are starving for love because everybody is in such a great rush.

ରଙ୍କ

FAITH IS A PRIVATE MATTER, USUALLY HELD DEEP WITHIN A PERSON, QUIET, IMPOSSIBLE TO RECOGNISE OR UNDERSTAND, IF YOU HAVE NO FAITH YOURSELF *Jennifer Worth*

ରଙ୍କ

For the Fallen

Binyon wrote 'For the Fallen in northern Cornwall in September 1914, just one month after the outbreak of the First World War

They shall grow not old,
as we that are left grow old:
Age shall not weary them,
nor the years condemn.
At the going down of the sun
and in the morning
We will remember them…

The Owl

I dimly perceive that whilst everything around me is ever changing, ever dying, there is underlying all that change a living power that is changeless, that holds all together, that creates, dissolves, and re-creates... in the midst of death life persists, in the midst of untruth truth persists, in the midst of darkness light persists.

Mahatma Ghandi

ଔ

Live life and let live,
enjoy,
be grateful,
don't waste time arguing,
fighting in doing bad things life is short,
live it,
be humble,
love yourself and be happy with what you have

Motherhood was the great equaliser for me;
I started to identify with everybody...
as a mother,
you have that impulse to wish that no child should ever be hurt,
or abused,
or go hungry,
or not have opportunities in life.

Annie Lennox

♋

IT'S SO MUCH DARKER
WHEN A LIGHT GOES OUT
THAN IT WOULD HAVE BEEN
IF IT HAD NEVER SHONE   *John Steinbeck*

♋

To One In Sorrow
Grace Noll Crowell

Let me come in where you are weeping, friend,
And let me take your hand.
I, who have known a sorrow such as yours,
Can understand.
Let me come in – I would be very still
Beside you in your grief;
I would not bid you cease your weeping, friend,
Tears can bring relief.
Let me come in – I would only breathe a prayer,
And hold your hand,
For I have known a sorrow such as yours,
And understand.

The fundamental love that a man needs in his life, if he is to have steady spiritual ease is the love of place where he was a child, and first became aware of the light, and the objects which the light illumined ... It is the hurt child become man that seeks the wilderness, wherein to rebuild himself.

Henry Williamson / Wilkinson

೧੪

What is so nice & so unexpected about life is the way it improves as it goes along. I think you should impress this fact on your children because I think young people have an awful feeling that life is slipping past them & they must do something – catch something – they don't quite know what, whereas they've only got to wait and it all comes.

Nancy Mitford

೧੪

Solitude is for me a fount of healing which makes my life worth living. Talking is often torment for me, and I need many days of silence to recover from the futility of words.

Carl Jung

೧੪

"It was only a sunny smile, and little it cost in the giving, but like morning light it scattered the night and made the day worth living."

F. Scott Fitzgerald

What is Prayer?

Prayer doesn't just happen when we kneel
or put hands together and focus and expect things from God
Instead…
Thinking positive and wishing good for others – That is prayer
When you hug a friend – That's a prayer
When you cook something to nourish family and friends - That's a prayer
When we send off our near and dear ones
and say 'Drive Safely' or 'Be Safe'- That's prayer
When you are helping someone in need by giving
your time and energy – You are praying
When you forgive someone by your heart …that is prayer.
Prayer is a Vibration - A feeling – A thought.
Prayer is the voice of love, friendship, genuine relationships.
Prayer is an expression of your silent self

ൠ

DARE
TO BE

The Gardener: Peace My Heart
Rabindranath Tagore

Peace, my heart, let the time for
the parting be sweet.
Let it not be a death but completeness.
Let love melt into memory and pain
into songs.

Let the flight through the sky end
in the folding of the wings over the
nest.
Let the last touch of your hands be
gentle like the flower of the night.

Stand still, 0 Beautiful End, for a
moment, and say your last words in
silence.
I bow to you and hold up my lamp
to light you on your way.

03

" Every bird, every tree,
every flower reminds
me what a blessing
and privilege it is
just to be alive"

Marty Rubin

"May the sun bring you new energy by day, may the moon softly restore you by night, may the rain wash away your worries, may the breeze blow new strength into your being, may you walk gently through the world and know it's beauty all the days of your life."

☙

We can never judge the lives of others, because each person knows only their own pain and renunciation. It's one thing to feel that you are on the right path, but it's another to think that yours is the only path.

Paulo Coelho

☙

"Words are our most inexhaustible source of magic, capable of both inflicting injury and remedying it"

JK Rowling - Dumbledore

☙

Some people could be given an entire field of roses and only see the thorns in it. Others could be given a single weed and only see the wildflower in it. Perception is a key component to gratitude. And gratitude a key component to joy.   *Amy Weatherly*

☙

"Why did you do all this for me?' he asked. 'I don't deserve it. I've never done anything for you.' 'You have been my friend,' replied Charlotte. 'That in itself is a tremendous thing."

E.B. White, Charlotte's Web

☙

There is a right and a wrong way of doing most things in life be they personal, or practical. Life is made up of opportunities few of which recur. Remain alert. What you do not wish done to yourself, do not do to others.

Confucius 551-479 BC

The Last Time

Anon

From the moment you hold your baby in your arms, you will
never be the same.
You might long for the person you were before, when you had
freedom and time and nothing in particular to worry about.
You will know tiredness like you never knew it before and days
will run into days that are exactly the same:
Full of feedings and burping, nappy changes and crying, whining
and fighting, naps or lack of naps
It might seem like a never-ending cycle.
But don't forget…
There is a last time for everything.
They will fall asleep on you after a long day, and it will be the last
time you ever hold your sleeping child.
One day you will carry them on your hip then set them down
and never pick them up that way again.
You will scrub their hair in the bath at night and from that day
on they will want to bathe alone.
They will hold your hand to cross the road then never reach for
it again.
They will creep into your room at midnight for cuddles and it
will be the last night you ever wake to this.
One afternoon you will sing "The Wheels on the Bus" and do all
the actions then never sing them that song again.
They will kiss you goodbye at the school gate then the next day
they will ask to walk to the gate alone.
You will read a final bedtime story and wipe your last dirty face.
They will run to you with arms raised for the very last time.
The thing is, you won't even know it's the last time until there are
no more times… and even then, it will take you a while to realise.
So while you are living in these times, remember there are only
so many of them and when they are gone, you will yearn for just
one more day of them.
For one last time.

THE GREATEST
OAK WAS ONCE
A LITTLE NUT THAT
HELD ITS GROUND

cx

Ambition should be to make the most of oneself, not only for one's
own sake but for one's family, friends and the world in general.
Never be too proud to listen to advice, remember, you need not
take it. Try not to indulge in self-pity; others will have even bigger
crosses to bear. Always carry a slate with you and write it regularly
clean of all grudges.

Sir Winston Churchill 1874-1965

cx

*A sense of humour
enhances life as also does a smile.
They cost nothing.
Use your mind as well as your emotions in
all important decisions, especially matters of the heart.*

Some day when you look back
Dhiman

Some day when you look back
To this day you will not
Look back at it with regret
But with comfort in your
Heart knowing tht even in
The most difficult of times,
When life challenged you at
Every step, you hung in
There and you did your best.
When you look back to this
Day I hope you will also
Remember those countless
Moments of courage and
Strength thst made you the
Person you are today

ଓ

*Half the battle in life
is to decide what is important and what is not.
Have a sense of priorities.
Reflect a lot
and then take action absolutely secure.*

Pope John Paul II, 1920-2005

"We may hold different points of view, but it is in times of stress and difficulty that we most need to remember that we have much more in common than there is dividing us"

Queen Elizabeth II

ം

What are heavy? sea-sand and sorrow.
What are brief? today and tomorrow.
What are frail? spring blossoms and youth.
What are deep? the ocean and truth.
Christina Rossetti

ം

If a child is to keep alive his inborn sense of wonder, he needs the companionship of at least one adult who can share it, rediscovering with him the joy, excitement, and mystery of the world we live in.

Rachel Carson

ം

Try and be an independent thinker. It is necessary if you are to keep your integrity. Make the best rather than the worst of people; it is right and rewarding to do so. Live as you are to die tomorrow, learn as if you are to live forever. *Erasmus of Rotterdam 1466-1536*

ം

Imagination and patience solve many problems. Always try and turn adversity to advantage, it usually can be, sometimes dramatically. Why use a five dollar word, when a ten cent will do. *Ernest Hemingway*

The Owl

Love knows not its own depth
until the hour of separation

☙

Just as treasures are uncovered from the earth,
so virtue appears from good deeds,
and wisdom appears from a pure and peaceful mind.
To walk safely through the maze of human life,
one needs the light of wisdom and the guidance of virtue.
Buddha

☙

In every walk with nature
one receives far more than he seeks.

John Muir

☙

We are such stuff
As dreams are made on,
and our little life
Is rounded with a sleep.

A garden to walk in
and immensity to dream in
– what more could he ask?
A few flowers at his feet
and above him the stars.
Victor Hugo

☙

FAITH IS THE BIRD THAT SINGS WHEN THE DAWN IS STILL DARK

Rabindranath Tagore

☙

Time is too slow for those who wait,
Too swift for those who fear,
too long for those who grieve,
Too short for those who rejoice,
but for those who love, time is eternity.
Henry Van Dyke

☙

And I think some suffering,
maybe even intense suffering,
is a necessary ingredient for life,
certainly for developing compassion.
Dalai Lama

☙

"I would like us all to stand shoulder to shoulder – metaphorically. Let's try not to get downhearted, we will get through this, whatever is thrown at us and together we can ensure that tomorrow will be a good day."
Captain Tom

A Fallen Limb *Anon*

A limb has fallen from the family tree.
I keep hearing a voice that says, "Grieve not for me.
Remember the best times, the laughter, the song.
The good life I lived while I was strong.
Continue my heritage, I'm counting on you.
Keep smiling and surely the sun will shine through.
My mind is at ease, my soul is at rest.
Remembering all, how I truly was blessed.
Continue traditions, no matter how small.
Go on with your life, don't worry about falls
I miss you all dearly, so keep up your chin.
Until the day comes we're together again."

ೞ

" I've learned that people will
forget what you said,
people will forget what you did,
but people will never forget
how you made them feel."

Maya Angelou

ೞ

It is not so much for its beauty
that the forest makes a claim upon men's hearts,
as for that subtle something, that quality of air,
that emanation from old trees,
that so wonderfully changes and renews a weary spirit.
Robert Louis Stevenson

YOUR HEART KNOWS THE WAY. RUN IN THAT DIRECTION.

Rumi

ᗉ

"Trees are the best monuments that a man can erect to his own memory.
They speak his praises without flattery,
and they are blessings to children yet unborn."
Lord Orrery, 1749

ᗉ

*A kind gesture can reach a wound
that only compassion can heal*

Steve Maraboli

ᗉ

Within tears, find hidden laughter
Seek treasures amid ruins, sincere one
Rumi

The Swallow **The Owl** The Sandpiper and The Little Red Robin   163

The Owl

Anxiety usually comes from strain, and strain
is caused by too complete a dependence on ourselves,
on our own devices, our own plans,
our own idea of what we are able to do.
Thomas Merton

ॐ

**Good men are not those who now and then do a good act,
but men who join one good act to another.**
Henry Ward Beecher

ॐ

In our age everything has to be a "problem".
Ours is a time of anxiety because we have willed it to be so.
Our anxiety is not imposed on us by force from outside.
We impose it on our world and upon one another
from within ourselves.

ॐ

**If you reveal your secrets to the wind,
you should not blame the wind for
revealing them to the trees.**
Kahlil Gibran

ॐ

"If you hear a voice within you say 'you cannot paint,'
then by all means paint,
and that voice will be silenced."
Vincent van Gogh

ॐ

**"Knowing your own darkness
is the best method for dealing
with the darknesses of other people."**
Carl Jung

Some grief shows
much of love,
But much of grief
shows still some
want of wit.

William Shakespeare, Romeo and Juliet

ೞ

"Raise your words, not voice.
It is rain that grows flowers, not thunder."
Rumi

ೞ

**When it hurts,
we return to the banks of certain rivers**
Czeslaw Milosz

ೞ

*Death leaves a heartache no one can heal,
love leaves a memory no one can steal.*
From an Irish headstone

The Owl

KIND WORDS CAN BE SHORT AND EASY TO SPEAK, BUT THEIR ECHOES ARE TRULY ENDLESS

Mother Teresa 1910-1997

☙

**A man of calm is like a shady tree.
People who need shelter come to it**

Toba Beta

☙

*It is a rough road
that leads to the heights of greatness*

Seneca

BUT WHAT IS STRONGER THAN THE HUMAN HEART WHICH SHATTERS OVER AND OVER AND LIVES

Rupi Kaur

ભ

Give the ones you love, wings to fly
Roots to come back,
And reasons to stay — *Dalai Lama*

ભ

Those who dream by day are cognizant of many things that escape those who dream only at night.

Edgar Allan Poe

The Owl

**What words of advice can your grandfather offer
after 80 years of unusually varied experience and fortune?
Well, here are twenty-one thoughts
which strike me as relevant to daily life
which I find useful and you might too.
Unless attributed they are my own**.

Half the battle in life is to decide what is important and what is not.
Have a sense of priorities.

Reflect a lot and then take action absolutely secure.
Pope John Paul 11, 1920-2005

Ambition should be to make the most of oneself, not only for one's own
sake but for one's family, friends and the world in general.

Never be too proud to listen to advice, remember, you need not take it.
Try not to indulge in self-pity; others will have even bigger crosses to bear.

Always carry a slate with you and write it regularly clean of all grudges
Sir Winston Churchill 1874-1965

Regardless of how much or how little money you may have,
it is a subject best talked about only selectively.

Be a good listener,
it will help you to develop an enquiring mind.

I think that one has to be ready to start all over again any number of times.
Abbot Herbert Byrne 1884-1978

Try and be an independent thinker.
It is necessary if you are to keep your integrity.
Make the best rather than the worst of people;
it is right and rewarding to do so.

Live as you are to die tomorrow,
learn as if you are to live forever.
Erasmus of Rotterdam 1466-1536

Imagination and patience solve many problems.
Always try and turn adversity to advantage,
it usually can be,
sometimes dramatically.

Why use a five dollar word, when a ten cent will do
Ernest Hemingway 1899-1961

There is a right and a wrong way of doing most things in life be they
personal, or practical.
Life is made up of opportunities few of which recur. Remain alert.

What you do not wish done to yourself, do not do to others.
Confucius 551-479 BC

A sense of humour enhances life as also does a smile.
They cost nothing. Use your mind as well as your emotions
in all important decisions, especially matters of the heart.

In short, there are three things that last;
FAITH, HOPE and LOVE,
and the greatest of these is LOVE.

Nicholas Fitzherbert to his grandson Ben, 2015

Fisherman's Ashes
Anon

Bear my ashes when I die
Far from men and let them lie,
By a salmon river.
Where the larches troop their ranks
And about the river banks
Silver Birches shiver.

Stay not stranger, passing by
For decorous lament or sigh
Where I rest beside you.
Go my brother, cast your line,
With a craft that once was mine
And good luck be tide you.

Here, who knows, I still may ply
O'er the stream a phantom fly
For a midnight capture.
And if Heaven attend my wish
Bring to bank a ghostly fish
In a ghostly rapture.

☙

*Solitary trees,
if they grow at all,
grow strong*

Winston Churchill

AND THEN
THE DAY CAME,
WHEN
THE RISK
TO REMAIN
TIGHT
IN A BUD
WAS MORE
PAINFUL
THAN THE RISK
IT TOOK
TO BLOSSOM

Anais Nin

The Sandpiper

spirit

c3

Your body is away from me
but there is a window open
from my heart to yours.

From this window, like the moon
I keep sending news secretly.

Rumi

Idyll

Siegfried Sassoon

In the grey summer garden I shall find you
With day-break and the morning hills behind you.
There will be rain-wet roses; stir of wings;
And down the wood a thrush that wakes and sings.
Not from the past you'll come, but from that deep
Where beauty murmurs to the soul asleep:
And I shall know the sense of life re-born
From dreams into the mystery of morn
Where gloom and brightness meet. And standing there
Till that calm song is done, at last we'll share
The league-spread, quiring symphonies that are
Joy in the world, and peace, and dawn's one star.

 భ

" You know that place between sleep and awake,
that place where you still remember dreaming?
That's where I'll always love you.
That's where I'll be waiting."

James V. Hart

ల

Life! We've been long together
Through pleasant and through cloudy weather;
Tis hard to part when friends are dear, - Perhaps 'twill cost a sigh, a tear.
Then steal away, give little warning.
Choose thine own time,
Say not "Good-night," but in some brighter clime,
Bid me "Good-morning."

Anna Laetitia Barbauld

IS IT POSSIBLE TO FEEL HOMESICK, NOT FOR A PLACE, BUT FOR A PERSON?

❧

God Has Not Promised Skies Always Blue *Anon*

God has not promised skies always blue,
Flower-strewn pathways all our lives through;
God has not promised sun without rain,
Joy without sorrow, peace without pain.
God has not promised we shall not bear
Many a burden, many a care.
He has not told us we shall not know
Toil and temptation, trouble and woe.
But God has promised strength for the day,
Rest for the labour, light for the way,
Grace for the trials, help from above,
Unfailing sympathy, undying love.

The Sandpiper

Stop all the clocks
W H Auden

Stop all the clocks, cut off the telephone,
Prevent the dog from barking with a juicy bone,
Silence the pianos and with muffled drum,
Bring out the coffin, let the mourners come.

Let aeroplanes circle moaning overhead,
Scribbling on the sky the message He Is Dead,
Put crepe bows round the white necks of the public doves,
Let the traffic policemen wear black cotton gloves.

He was my North, my South, my East and West,
My working week and my Sunday rest,
My noon, my midnight, my talk, my song;
I thought that love would last for ever: I was wrong.

The stars are not wanted now: put out every one;
Pack up the moon and dismantle the sun;
Pour away the ocean and sweep up the wood;
For nothing now can ever come to any good.

☙

TO THRIVE IN LIFE YOU NEED THREE BONES: A WISHBONE A BACKBONE AND A FUNNY BONE

☙

I never know what people mean when they complain of loneliness.
To be alone is one of life's greatest delights, thinking one's own
thoughts, doing one's own little jobs, seeing the world beyond and
feeling oneself uninterrupted in the rooted connection with the
centre of all things.
D. H. Lawrence

176

My Way
Frank Sinatra

Regrets, I've had a few
But then again, too few to mention
I did what I had to do and saw it through without exemption
I planned each charted course, each careful step along the byway
And more, much more than this, I did it my way

I've loved, I've laughed and cried
I've had my fill, my share of losing
And now, as tears subside, I find it all so amusing
To think I did all that
And may I say, not in a shy way,
"Oh, no, oh, no, not me, I did it my way"

☙

*You may forget with whom you laughed,
but you will never forget with whom you wept*

Kahlil Gibran

☙

Hogmanay

Haste ye back, I love you dearly,
Call again, you're welcome here.
May your days be free from sorrow and your friends be ever near.

May the paths o'er which you wander
Be a joy to you each day.
Haste ye back, I love you dearly,
Haste ye back on friendship's way.

The Sandpiper

The Sound of Silence
Paul Simon

And in the naked light, I saw
Ten thousand people, maybe more
People talking without speaking
People hearing without listening
People writing songs that voices never shared
And no one dared
Disturb the sound of silence
"Fools" said I, "You do not know
Silence like a cancer grows
Hear my words that I might teach you
Take my arms that I might reach you"

ᴄꙅ

Gone Fishing
by Delmar Pepper

I've finished life's chores assigned to me,
So put me on a boat headed out to sea.
Please send along my fishing pole
For I've been invited to the fishin' hole.

> **Where every day is a day to fish,**
> To fill your heart with every wish.
> **Don't worry, or feel sad for me,**
> I'm fishin' with the Master of the sea.
> **We will miss each other for awhile,**
> But you will come and bring your smile.
> **That won't be long you will see,**
> Till we're together you and me.

To all of those that think of me,
Be happy as I go out to sea.
If others wonder why I'm missin',
Just tell 'em I've gone fishin'

God Saw You Getting Tired
Anon

God saw you getting tired
When a cure was not to be.
So He wrapped His arms around you,
And whispered, "Come unto me".
You didn't deserve what you went through,
And so He gave you rest.
God's garden must be beautiful,
He only takes the best.
So when I saw you sleeping,
So peaceful and free from pain.
I could not wish you to come back,
to suffer that all again.

❧

*If only our eyes saw souls instead of bodies,
how different would our ideals of beauty be.*

❧

What is the difference between

I like you and
I love you

Beautifully answered by Buddha:

when you **like** a flower, you just pluck it.
But when you **love** a flower, you water it daily…

Ask My Mum How She Is

My Mum, she tells a lot of lies, she never did before
But from now until she dies, she'll tell a whole lot more.

Ask my Mum how she is, and because she can't explain,
She will tell a little lie because she can't describe the pain.

Ask my Mum how she is, she'll say "I'm alright."
If that's the truth, then tell me, why does she cry each night?

Ask my Mum how she is, she seems to cope so well,
She didn't have a choice you see, nor the strength to yell.

Ask my Mum how she is, "I'm fine, I'm well, I'm coping."
For God's sake Mum, just tell the truth, just say your heart is broken.

She'll love me all her life, I loved her all of mine.
But if you ask her how she is, she'll lie and say she's fine.

I am here in Heaven, I cannot hug from here.
If she lies to you don't listen, hug her and hold her near.

On the day we meet again, we'll smile and I'll be bold.
I'll say, "You're lucky to get in here, Mum,
With all the lies you told!"

cx

A wise physician once said,
'The best medicine for humans is love.'
Someone asked, 'What if it doesn't work?'
He smiled and answered,
'Increase the dose'.

The Crescent Moon
Amy Lowell - 1874-1925

Slipping softly through the sky
Little horned, happy moon,
Can you hear me up so high?
Will you come down soon?

On my nursery window-sill
Will you stay your steady flight?
And then float away with me
Through the summer night?

Brushing over tops of trees,
Playing hide and seek with stars,
Peeping up through shiny clouds
At Jupiter or Mars.

I shall fill my lap with roses
Gathered in the milky way,
All to carry home to mother.
Oh! what will she say!

Little rocking, sailing moon,
Do you hear me shout — Ahoy!
Just a little nearer, moon,
To please a little boy.

❧

Inside Our Dreams
Jeanne Willis

Where do people go to when they die?
Somewhere down below or in the sky?
'I can't be sure,' said Grandad, 'but it seems
They simply set up home inside our dreams.'

Granny's Button Box

I maun sort oot this button box noo Gran his gaen tae rest.
She'd niver throw ev'n ane awa frae suit or coat or dress,
bit pit them a' in this aul box, fur losh! Ye niver ken
the day they'd come in handy fur shewin on again.
Guid sakes, there maun be hunners here, a' colours, shapes an' size.
I'm shair they're better thrown awa, keepin them widna be wise.
They dinna match wi' onythin' that we fowk wear the day.
Na, na! The scaffie'll tak them awa, nae maitter fit ya say.
Bit wait a meenit! See this here? That wis aff her waddin suit,
an this ane here I mind fine, come aff me buttoned boot.
My! here's the hook she uset tae cleek each button intae place,
while I'd sit there, a wee bit lass, a soor look on me face.
Noo this lot here a' tied wi' string, wis aff ma velvet coat.
I couldna hae been much mair than five, gaun doon tae meet Da's boat.
There wis a hat that gaed tae match. Oh aye, I mind that fine.
Jist fancy her hingin on tae them efter a' this time!
See this bonny crystal ane fair glintin in the licht!
That wis aff a frock I wore tae a waddin. Fit a sicht!
A' crêpe de chine an' frills an' things, an' them a' room the neck.
Nae diamond iver shone as bricht as I did in the kirk.
She shewed them on bi gas licht, each ane pit on wi' care.
Working awa wi' lovin hauns until her een wir saur.
Noo this big black ane I ken fine, cam aff Da's fishin breeks.
He wis a deep sea fisherman I didna see fur weeks.
This rubber ane's aff hes woollen drawers! She knittit a' the while.
The yarns o' wool that she uset up main hae stretch't fur monys a mile.
Here's ane come aff ma first dance frock. Hmm That wis gay lang syne.
An look at this aff ma gym slip fin I wis only nine.
An Army ane aff the tunic I wore fin in the war.
I jinet tae dae ma little bit tae bring the peace wance more.
She grat the day I gaed awa, an' tell't me tac tak care,
fur I wis her only lassie an naebidy looed me mair.
Here's bits an' bobs frae ma ane bairns' claes, she shewed fur them an' a'.
Knittin vests an socks tae keep them warm fin the winters wins did blaw.

I c'n see there's mair than buttons here, bit memories she loved tae keep.
She's left them a' tae me noo she's gaen tae her last sleep.
Fit? Throw them oot! Na na, that's mair than I c'n dee.
I'll jist pit them in this button box that noo belangs tae me.
Fur I c'n see, that jist like Gran, a hoarder I am tae.
Wi' a box jist fu' o' memories I'll keep till ma last day.

☙

EVEN THE DARKEST NIGHT WILL END AND THE SUN WILL RISE

Victor Hugo, Les Misérables

☙

The Tempest
Francis Quarles

A grandmother is a lady who has no children of her own, so she likes other people's little girls. A grandfather is a man grandmother. He goes walks with the boys and they talk about fishing, and tractors. Grandmothers don't have to do anything but be there. They are old, so they shouldn't play hard or run. They never say "hurry up". They are often fat, but not too fat to tie children's shoes. They don't have to be clever, only answer question like why dogs don't like cats and why god isn't married. They don't talk baby talk like visitors. When they read to us they don't skip bits or mind if it is the same story over again.

Good Times *Anon*

When I grew up I walked to school and our tea time was at a regular time, Sunday lunch was chicken and all the trimmings, we all sat down at a table and used our knives and forks correctly with no elbows on the table.

We only received a toy on birthdays and at Christmas.

Fast food was fish and chips for tea on a Friday and having a bottle of Corona pop from the shop was a real treat.

You took your school clothes off as soon as you got home and put on your 'playing out' clothes. Children looked like children, we didn't pout, wear makeup or have anxiety. There was no taking or picking you up in the car, you walked or rode your bike if you had one and bunked off. There was no such things as private conversations or mobile phones, even the landline was attached to the wall!

We didn't have Now TV, Sky or Netflix, we had only 3 channels to watch. we had to watch all of the adverts unless you switched to BBC. We played army bull dog, peep behind the curtain, kerby, hide and seek, tag, football, we made mud pies and rode bikes.

Staying in the house was a PUNISHMENT and the only thing we knew about "bored" was, "You better find something to do before I find it for you!"

We ate what mum made for our tea or we ate nothing at all. If we rushed our tea we weren't allowed to go back out and if we didn't eat it we weren't allowed back out either

Bottled water was not a thing; we drank from the tap. Council juice.

We watched cartoons on Saturday mornings, and rode our bikes for hours and ran around. We weren't AFRAID OF ANYTHING. We played till dark... street lights were our alarm.

If someone had a fight, that's what it was and we were friends again a week later, if not SOONER.

We watched our mouths around our elders because all of our aunts, uncles, grandpas, grandma's and our parents' best friends were all extensions of our parents and you didn't want them telling your parents if you misbehaved! Or they would give you something to cry about. Everyone had respect. I still don't argue with older people and always give up my seat

I did my research by borrowing books from the library. There was no internet and no Google!

These were the good old days. So many kids today will never know how it feels to be a real kid. I loved my childhood and all the mates I hung around with. Good Times.

❧

I Worried a Lot
Mary Oliver

I worried a lot. Will the garden grow, will the rivers
flow in the right direction, will the earth turn
as it was taught, and if not how shall I correct it?

Was I right, was I wrong, will I be forgiven, can I do better?
Will I ever be able to sing, even the sparrows
can do it and I am, well, hopeless.

Is my eyesight fading or am I just imagining it,
am I going to get rheumatism, lockjaw, dementia?
Finally, I saw that worrying had come to nothing.
And gave it up.
And took my old body and went out into the morning,
and sang.

 The Sandpiper

Why Me?
Barbara Vance

If you have to ask Why me?
When you're feeling really blue,
When the world has turned against you
And you don't know what to do,
When it pours colossal raindrops,
And the road's a winding mess,
And you're feeling more confused
Than you ever could express,
When the saddened sun won't shine,
When the stars will not align,
When you'd rather be
Inside your bed,
The covers pulled
Above your head,
When life is something
That you dread,
And you have to ask Why me? . . .
Then when the world seems right and true,
When rain has left a gentle dew,
When you feel happy being you,
Please ask yourself, why me? then, too.

℃

DON'T CRY BECAUSE IT IS OVER; SMILE BECAUSE IT HAPPENED.

Dr Seuss

*Let my thoughts come to you, when I am gone,
like the afterglow of sunset at the margin of starry silence*

☙

That Song Came on Today
Bernard O'Donague

That song came on today,
The one you loved.
The one we listened to together,
The one whose melody mingles
With so many of our memories
A soundtrack in the background of our days.

That song came on today.
The one that stops me in my tracks.
The one I have to skip sometimes
The one that sings about you
in so many ways.

That song came on today,
The one that hurts my heart to hear.
The one that lives deep in my core.
The one that transports me back to you.

But, that song came on today,
The one you loved.
And I sang along.
Some days,
I can sing along.
I hope you're singing too.

An Ode to A Sunflower

Sophie MacAulay
in memory of her mother (Henrietta) and her sister (Joanna) 2021

Oh joyous sunflower!
The queen of all flowers,
There is no other with you that can compare,
The roadside and fields are made golden
Because your bright presence is there.
Above all the weeds that surround you
You raise to the sun your bright head,
Embroidering beautiful landscapes,
Bringing golden light to all others in the bed.

Oh queen of the September morning
You watch for the first ray of sun,
And salute the bright orb as it travels
Until the bright day of autumn is done.
Tho' difficulty may arise in the pasture
And the floods may flow in the field,
You continue to bring joy and sunshine
To every seed in the future years yield.

So there she is,
such a glorious one,
peeping over the fences ahead,
She covers the hillsides with gold,
Even when her petals have shed.
So, my dear Sunflower, grow tall in the meadows beyond,
And spread your arms to the breezes,
Holding tight to our indestructible bond.

Those times that I have pondered on wherever you may be,
I know now that your presence is beyond where the eye can see.
So I thank you, my dear Sunflower, for all the radiance you still bring
To me, today and every day,

Going Without Saying
Bernard O'Donoghue

It is a great pity we don't know
When the dead are going to die
So that, over a last companionable
Drink, we could tell them
How much we liked them.
Happy the man who, dying, can
Place his hand on his heart and say:
'At least I didn't neglect to tell
The thrush how beautifully she sings.'

&

Don't prioritise your looks my friend
Donna Ashworth

Don't prioritise your looks my friend, they won't last the journey.
Your sense of humour though, will only get better.
Your intuition will grow and expand like a majestic
cloak of wisdom.
Your ability to choose your battles,
will be fine-tuned to perfection.
Your capacity for stillness, for living in the moment, will blossom.
And your desire to live each and every moment will transcend
all other wants.
Your instinct for knowing what (and who) is worth your time,
will grow and flourish like ivy on a castle wall.
Don't prioritise your looks my friend,
they will change forevermore,
that pursuit is one of much sadness and disappointment.
Prioritise the uniqueness that makes you you,
and the invisible magnet that draws in other like-minded souls
to dance in your orbit.
These are the things which will only get better.

Welcome to Holland
Emily Perl Kingsley

When you're going to have a baby, it's like you're planning a vacation to Italy. You're all excited. You get a whole bunch of guidebooks, you learn a few phrases so you can get around, and then it comes time to pack your bags and head for the airport.

Only when you land, the stewardess says, "Welcome to Holland."

You look at one another in disbelief and shock, saying, "Holland? What are you talking about? I signed up for Italy." But they explain that there's been a change of plan, that you've landed in Holland and there you must stay.

"But I don't kow anything about Holland!" you say. 'I don't want to stay!"

But stay, you do.

You go out and buy some new guidebooks, you learn some new phrases, and you meet people you never knew existed. The important thing is that you are not in a bad place filled with despair. You're simply in a different place than you had planned.

It's slower paced than Italy, less flashy than Italy, but after you've been there a little while and you have a chance to catch your breath, you begin to discover that Holland has windmills. Holland has tulips. Holland has Rembrandts.

But everyone else you know is busy coming and going from Italy. They're all bragging about what a great time they had there, and for the rest of your life, you'll say, "Yes, that's what I had planned."

The pain of that will never go away.

You have to accept that pain, because the loss of that dream, the loss of that plan, is a very, very significant loss.

But if you spend your life mourning the fact that you didn't get to go to Italy, you will never be free to enjoy the very special, the very lovely things about Holland.

When Children Respected what Older Folks Said
Anon

When children respected what older folks said,
and pot was a thing you kept under your bed.
Back in the days of *Listen with Mother*,
when neighbours were friendly and talked to each other.
When cars were so rare you could play in the street.
When Doctors made house calls; Police walked the beat.
Back in the days of Milligan's Goons,
when butter was butter and songs all had tunes.
It was dumplings for dinner and trifle for tea,
and your annual break was a day by the sea.
Back in the days of *Dixon of Dock Green*,
Crackerjack pens and Lyons ice cream.
When children could freely wear National Health glasses,
and teachers all stood at the front of their classes.
Back in the days of rocking and reeling,
when mobiles were things that you hung from the ceiling.
When woodwork and pottery got taught in schools,
and everyone dreamed of a win on the pools.
Back in the days when I was a lad,
I can't help but smile for the fun that I had.
Hopscotch and roller skates; snowballs to lob.
Back in the days of tanners and bobs.

ଓଃ

And I will love thee still, my dear,
Till a' the seas gang dry

Only Once in Your Life...

Only once in your life, I truly believe, you find someone who can completely turn your world around. You tell them things that you've never shared with another soul and they absorb everything you say and actually want to hear more. You share hopes for the future, dreams that will never come true, goals that were never achieved and the many disappointments life has thrown at you. When something wonderful happens, you can't wait to tell them about it, knowing they will share in your excitement. They are not embarrassed to cry with you when you are hurting or laugh with you when you make a fool of yourself. Never do they hurt your feelings or make you feel like you are not good enough, but rather they build you up and show you the things about yourself that make you special and even beautiful. There is never any pressure, jealousy or competition but only a quiet calmness when they are around. You can be yourself and not worry about what they will think of you because they love you for who you are. The things that seem insignificant to most people such as a note, song or walk become invaluable treasures kept safe in your heart to cherish forever. Memories of your childhood come back and are so clear and vivid it's like being young again. Colours seem brighter and more brilliant. Laughter seems part of daily life where before it was infrequent or didn't exist at all. A phone call or two during the day helps to get you through a long day's work and always brings a smile to your face. In their presence, there's no need for continuous conversation, but you find you're quite content in just having them nearby. Things that never interested you before become fascinating because you know they are important to this person who is so special to you. You think of this person on every occasion and in everything you do. Simple things bring them to mind like a pale blue sky, gentle wind or even a storm cloud on the horizon. You open your heart knowing that there's a chance it may be broken one day and in opening your heart, you experience a love and joy that you never dreamed possible. You find that being vulnerable is the only way to allow your heart to feel true pleasure that's so real it scares you. You find strength in knowing you have a true friend and possibly a soul mate who will remain loyal to the end. Life seems completely different, exciting and worthwhile. Your only hope and security is in knowing that they are a part of your life.

Bob Marley

192

My Shadow
Robert Louis Stevenson

I have a little shadow that goes in and out with me,
And what can be the use of him is more than I can see.
He is very, very like me from the heels up to the head;
And I see him jump before me, when I jump into my bed.

The funniest thing about him is the way he likes to grow –
Not at all like proper children, which is always very slow;
For he sometimes shoots up taller like an india-rubber ball,
And he sometimes gets so little that there's none of him at all.

He hasn't got a notion of how children ought to play,
And can only make a fool of me in every sort of way.
He stays so close beside me, he's a coward you can see;
I'd think shame to stick to nursie as that shadow sticks to me!

One morning, very early, before the sun was up,
I rose and found the shining dew on every buttercup;
But my lazy little shadow, like an arrant sleepy-head,
Had stayed at home behind me and was fast asleep in bed.

❧

" Oh, you tears,
I'm thankful that you run.
Though you trickle in the darkness,
You shall glitter in the sun.
The rainbow could not shine if the rain
refused to fall;
And the eyes that cannot weep
are the saddest eyes of all." *Charles Mackay*

The Sandpiper

A nurse took the tired, anxious serviceman to the bedside...

A nurse took the tired, anxious serviceman to the bedside. "Your son is here," she said to the old man. She had to repeat the words several times before the patient's eyes opened.

Heavily sedated because of the pain of his heart attack, he dimly saw the young uniformed Marine standing outside the oxygen tent. He reached out his hand. The Marine wrapped his toughened fingers around the old man's limp ones, squeezing a message of love and encouragement.

The nurse brought a chair so that the Marine could sit beside the bed. All through the night the young Marine sat there in the poorly lighted ward, holding the old man's hand and offering him words of love and strength. Occasionally, the nurse suggested that the Marine move away and rest awhile. He refused.

Whenever the nurse came into the ward, the Marine was oblivious of her and of the night noises of the hospital – the clanking of the oxygen tank, the laughter of the night staff members exchanging greetings, the cries and moans of the other patients. Now and then she heard him say a few gentle words. The dying man said nothing, only held tightly to his son all through the night.

Along towards dawn, the old man died. The Marine released the now lifeless hand he had been holding and went to tell the nurse. While she did what she had to do, he waited.

Finally, she returned. She started to offer words of sympathy, but the Marine interrupted her, "Who was that man?" he asked.

The nurse was startled, "He was your father," she answered.

"No, he wasn't," the Marine replied. "I never saw him before in my life."

"Then why didn't you say something when I took you to him?"

"I knew right away there had been a mistake, but I also knew he needed his son, and his son just wasn't here. When I realised that he was too sick to tell whether or not I was his son, knowing how much he needed me, I stayed. I came here tonight to find a Mr. William Grey. His Son was killed in Iraq today, and I was sent to inform him. What was this Gentleman's Name? "

The nurse with tears in her eyes answered, "Mr. William Grey..."

Roy Popkin

ॐ

WEEPING IS NOT THE SAME THING AS CRYING. IT TAKES YOUR WHOLE BODY TO WEEP, AND WHEN IT'S OVER, YOU FEEL LIKE YOU DON'T HAVE ANY BONES LEFT TO HOLD YOU UP.

Sarah Ockler

ॐ

I Often Say Rugby's Like Life

"I often say rugby's like life. You can have the ball in your hand and be running down the field feeling unstoppable. Then someone tackles you and you hit the deck and you're vulnerable; you're lying there exposed. Suddenly your team-mates are there, not just over the ball but over you, protecting you. They're prepared to put their bodies on the line for you. That's what happens in life: you fall over and your mates come to your aid."

Sir John Kirwan

The Sandpiper

The Call of Africa
C Emily-Dibb

When you've acquired a taste for dust,
And the scent of our first rain,
You're hooked for life on Africa,
And you'll not be right again.
Until you can watch the setting moon
And hear the jackals bark,
And know that they're around you,
Waiting in the dark.

When you long to see the elephants
Or to hear the coucal's song,
When the moonrise sets your blood on fire,
Then you've been away too long.
It's time to cut the traces loose,
And let your heart go free,
Beyond that far horizon,
Where your spirit yearns to be.

Africa is waiting – come!
Since you've touched the open sky
And learned to love the rustling grass,
And the wild fish eagle's cry,
You'll always hunger for the bush;
For the lion's rasping roar,
To camp at last beneath the stars
And to be at peace once more.

മ

Nothing about human beings ever had the power to move me as a child. Black Beauty now …!

Nancy Mitford

It is Also Then that I Wish I Believed...
Hanya Yanagihara, A Little Life

"It is also then that I wish I believed in some sort of life after life, that in another universe, maybe on a small red planet where we have not legs but tails, where we paddle through the atmosphere like seals, where the air itself is sustenance, composed of trillions of molecules of protein and sugar and all one has to do is open one's mouth and inhale in order to remain alive and healthy, maybe you two are there together, floating through the climate. Or maybe he is closer still: maybe he is that gray cat that has begun to sit outside our neighbour's house, purring when I reach out my hand to it; maybe he is that new puppy I see tugging at the end of my other neighbour's leash; maybe he is that toddler I saw running through the square a few months ago, shrieking with joy, his parents huffing after him; maybe he is that flower that suddenly bloomed on the rhododendron bush I thought had died long ago; maybe he is that cloud, that wave, that rain, that mist. It isn't only that he died, or how he died; it is what he died believing. And so I try to be kind to everything I see, and in everything I see, I see him."

❧

The Tale of Two Wolves

An old Cherokee is teaching his grandson about life.
"A fight is going on inside me," he said to the boy.
"It is a terrible fight and it is between two wolves. One is evil – he is anger, envy, sorrow, regret, greed, arrogance, self-pity, guilt, resentment, inferiority, lies, false pride, superiority, and ego." He continued, "The other is good – he is joy, peace, love, hope, serenity, humility, kindness, benevolence, empathy, generosity, truth, compassion, and faith. The same fight is going on inside you – and inside every other person, too."
The grandson thought about it for a minute and then asked his grandfather, "Which wolf will win?"
The old Cherokee simply replied, "The one you feed."

Who Will Take Grandma
Clara Clark-Grantz

Who will take grandma? Who will it be?
All of us *want* her, – I'm sure you'll agree!
Let's call a meeting, – let's gather the clan,
Let's get it settled as soon as we can.

> In such a big family there's certainly one
> Willing to give her a place in the sun!
> Strange how we thought that she'd never wear out,
> But see how she walks, it's arthritis, no doubt,

Her eyesight is faded, her memory's dim,
She's apt to insist on the silliest whim,
When people get older they become such a care!
She must have a home, but the question is where?

> Remember the days when she used to be spry?
> Baked her own cookies and made her own pie?
> Helped us with lessons and tended our seams,
> Kissed away troubles and mended our dreams?

Wonderful Grandma! We all loved her so!
Isn't it dreadful she's no place to go?
One little corner is all she would need,
A shoulder to cry on, her Bible to read,

> A chair by the window with sun coming through,
> Some pretty spring flowers still covered with dew,
> Who'll warm her with love so she won't mind the cold?
> Oh, who will take Grandmother now that she's old?

What? Nobody wants her? Oh, yes, there is *one*
Willing to give her a place in the sun,
Where she won't have to worry or wonder or doubt,
And she won't be *our* problem to bother about,

Pretty soon now, God will give her a bed,
But who'll dry our tears when dear Grandma is dead?

The Wild Geese

Violet Jacob (1863 - 1946), who wrote this poem, was born Violet Kennedy-Erskine into an aristocratic family near Montrose, Angus. She is known best for her historical novel Flemington *and her poetry. In 1894 she married an Irish officer in the British Army, and accompanied him to India where he was serving. When Arthur died in 1936, she returned to live at Kirriemuir, in Angus. Although the poem is ostensibly a conversation between the wind and a wild goose, it is clearly also about being an exile - feelings that Violet Jacob must have felt when she was in India.*

'Oh, tell me what was on yer road, ye roarin' norlan
    As ye cam' blawin' frae the land that's niver frae my mind?
My feet they trayvel England, but I'm deein' for the north –'
    'My man, I heard the siller tides rin up the Firth o' Forth.'
'Aye, Wind, I ken them well eneuch, and fine they fa' and rise,
    And fain I'd feel the creepin' mist on yonder shore that lies,
But tell me, ere ye passed them by, what saw ye on the way ?'
    'My man, I rocked the rovin' gulls that sail abune the Tay.'
'But saw ye naethin', leein' Wind, afore ye cam' to Fife?
    There's muckle lyin' yont the Tay that's mair to me nor life.'
'My man, I swept the Angus braes ye haena trod for years –'
    'O Wind, forgie a hameless loon that canna see for tears! –'
'And far abune the Angus straths I saw the wild geese flee,
    A lang, lang skein o' beatin' wings wi' their heids towards the sea,
And aye their cryin' voices trailed ahint them on the air –'
    'O Wind, hae maircy, haud yer whisht, for I daurna listen mair!'

> *norlan = someone who lives in the north*
> *fain = fondly*
> *abune = above*
> *muckle = a lot*
> *yont = beyond*
> *hameless loon = homeless lad*
> *straths = valleys, glens*
> *haud yer whisht = keep quiet!*
> *daurna listen mair = dare not listen more*

The World Grows Better Year by Year
Mildred Bain, 1930

The world grows better year by year
Because some nurse in her little sphere,
Puts on her apron, smiles and sings
And keeps on doing the same old things.

> Taking the temperature, giving the pills
> To remedy mankind's numerous ills
> Feeding the baby, answering the bells
> Being polite with a heart that rebels.

Longing for home and all the while
Wearing the same old professional smile
Blessing the new-born babes first breath
Closing the eyes that are still in death

> Taking the blame for the doctor's mistakes
> Oh dear, what a lot of patience it takes
> Going off duty at seven o' clock
> Tired discouraged and ready to drop

But called back on special at seven fifteen
With woe in her heart, but it must not be seen
Morning and evening and noon and night
Just doing it over and hoping its right.

> When we lay down our caps and cross the bar,
> Oh Lord will you give us just one little star
> To wear in our crowns without uniforms new
> In that city above where that Head Nurse is You

☙

This is the time to be slow
John O'Donohue

This is the time to be slow,
Lie low to the wall
Until the bitter weather passes.

Try, as best you can, not to let
The wire brush of doubt
Scrape from your heart
All sense of yourself
And your hesitant light.

If you remain generous,
Time will come good;
And you will find your feet
Again on fresh pastures of promise,
Where the air will be kind
And blushed with beginning.

☙

I DREAMED I WAS A BUTTERFLY,
FLITTING AROUND IN THE SKY;
THEN I AWOKE.
NOW I WONDER:
AM I A MAN WHO DREAMT OF
BEING A BUTTERFLY,
OR AM I A BUTTERFLY
DREAMING THAT I AM A MAN?

Zhuangzi

The Sandpiper

I've tried the high-toned specialists
Edgar Guest

I've tried the high-toned specialists, who doctor folks today;
I've heard the throat man whisper low "Come on now let us spray";
I've sat in fancy offices and waited long my turn,
And paid for fifteen minutes what it took a week to earn;
But while these scientific men are kindly, one and all,
I miss the good old doctor that my mother used to call.
The old-time family doctor! Oh, I am sorry that he's gone,
He ushered us into the world and knew us every one;
He didn't have to ask a lot of questions, for he knew
Our histories from birth and all the ailments we'd been through.
And though as children small, we feared the medicines he'd send,
The old-time family doctor grew to be our dearest friend.
No hour too late, no night too rough for him to heed our call;
He knew exactly where to hang his coat up in the hall;
He knew exactly where to go, which room upstairs to find
The patient he'd been called to see, and saying: "Never mind,
I'll run up there myself and see what's causing all the fuss."
It seems we grew to look and lean on him as one of us.
He had a big and kindly heart, a fine and tender way,
And more than once I've wished that I could call him in today.
The specialists are clever men and busy men, I know,
And haven't time to doctor as they did long years ago;
But some day he may come again, the friend that we can call,
The good old family doctor who will love us one and all.

❦

*A flock of geese leave their lake and take wing,
turning to poems in the sky.*
Dr. Sun Wolf

Close the Gate
Nancy Kraayenhof

For this one farmer the worries are over,
       lie down and rest your head,
Your time has been and struggles enough,
       put the tractor in the shed.
Years were not easy, many downright hard,
       but your faith in God transcended,
Put away your tools and sleep in peace.
       The fences have all been mended.
You raised a fine family, worked the land well
       and always followed the Son,
Hang up your shovel inside of the barn;
       your work here on earth is done.
A faith few possess led your journey through life,
       often a jagged and stony way,
The sun is setting, the cattle are all bedded,
       and here now is the end of your day.
Your love of God's soil has passed on to your kin;
       the stories flow like fine wine,
Wash off your work boots in the puddle
       left by blessed rain one final time.
You always believed that the good Lord would provide
       and He always had somehow,
Take off your gloves and put them down,
       no more sweat and worry for you now.
Your labour is done, your home now is heaven;
       no more must you wait,
Your legacy lives on, your love of the land,
       and we will close the gate.

ᵃ

The Trouble Tree

I hired a plumber to help me restore an old farmhouse, and after he had just finished a rough first day on the job: a flat tyre made him lose an hour of work, his electric drill quit and his ancient one ton truck refused to start. While I drove him home, he sat in stony silence. On arriving, he invited me in to meet his family. As we walked toward the front door, he paused briefly at a small tree, touching the tips of the branches with both hands. When opening the door he underwent an amazing transformation. His face was wreathed in smiles and he hugged his two small children and gave his wife a kiss. Afterward he walked me to the car. We passed the tree and my curiosity got the better of me. I asked him about what I had seen him do earlier. 'Oh, that's my trouble tree,' he replied 'I know I can't help having troubles on the job, but one thing's for sure, those troubles don't belong in the house with my wife and the children. So I just hang them up on the tree every night when I come home and ask God to take care of them. Then in the morning I pick them up again. Funny thing is,' he smiled, 'when I come out in the morning to pick 'em up, there aren't nearly as many as I remember hanging up the night before.'

cs

Earth and sky, woods and fields,
lakes and rivers, the mountain and the sea,
are excellent schoolmasters,
and teach some of us more than we can ever learn
from books.

John Lubbock

Bird of the sky,
How does it feel to dart and fly,
How does it feel to soar all day
"Over the hills and far away"?
To live in a tree,
To build a house as fine
    as can be,
To build it safe, and warm,
    and high,
And call it home – bird of the sky?
To perch and sing,
Up there where the leaves
    are quivering,
Singing and winging and
    building high,
How does it feel – bird of the sky?

Annette Wynne

*The Sandpiper*

In the Circus Queue
Katharine Hepburn

Once when I was a teenager, my father and I were standing in line to buy tickets for the circus.

Eventually, there was only one other family between us and the ticket counter. This family made a big impression on me.

There were eight children, all probably under the age of 12. The way they were dressed, you could tell they didn't have a lot of money, but their clothes were neat and clean.

The children were well-behaved, all of them standing in line, two-by-two behind their parents, holding hands. They were excitedly jabbering about the clowns, animals, and all the acts they would be seeing that night. By their excitement you could sense they had never been to the circus before. It would be a highlight of their lives.

The father and mother were at the head of the pack standing proud as could be. The mother was holding her husband's hand, looking up at him as if to say, "You're my knight in shining armour." He was smiling and enjoying seeing his family happy.

The ticket lady asked the man how many tickets he wanted? He proudly responded, "I'd like to buy eight children's tickets and two adult tickets, so I can take my family to the circus." The ticket lady stated the price.

The man's wife let go of his hand, her head dropped, the man's lip began to quiver. Then he leaned a little closer and asked, "How much did you say?" The ticket lady again stated the price.

The man didn't have enough money. How was he supposed to turn and tell his eight kids that he didn't have enough money to take them to the circus?

Seeing what was going on, my dad reached into his pocket, pulled out a £20 note, and then dropped it on the ground. (We were not wealthy in any sense of the word!) My father bent down, picked up the £20 note, tapped the man on the shoulder and said, "Excuse me, sir, this fell out of your pocket."

The man understood what was going on. He wasn't begging

for a handout but certainly appreciated the help in a desperate, heartbreaking and embarrassing situation.

He looked straight into my dad's eyes, took my dad's hand in both of his, squeezed tightly onto the £20 note, and with his lip quivering and a tear streaming down his cheek, he replied; "Thank you, thank you, sir. This really means a lot to me and my family."

My father and I went back to our car and drove home. The £20 that my dad gave away is what we were going to buy our own tickets with.

Although we didn't get to see the circus that night, we both felt a joy inside us that was far greater than seeing the circus could ever provide.

That day I learnt the value to Give.

℘

The Bright Field
R. S. Thomas

> I have seen the sun break through
> to illuminate a small field
> for a while, and gone my way
> and forgotten it. But that was the
> pearl of great price, the one field that had
> treasure in it. I realise now
> that I must give all that I have
> to possess it. Life is not hurrying
> on to a receding future, nor hankering after
> an imagined past. It is the turning
> aside like Moses to the miracle
> of the lit bush, to a brightness
> that seemed as transitory as your youth
> once, but is the eternity that awaits you.

Tell Me
Nick Trout

It may be a cat, a bird, a ferret, or a guinea pig, but the chances are high that when someone close to you dies, a pet will be there to pick up the slack. Pets devour the loneliness. They give us purpose, responsibility, a reason for getting up in the morning, and a reason to look to the future. They ground us, help us escape the grief, make us laugh, and take full advantage of our weakness by exploiting our furniture, our beds, and our refrigerator. We wouldn't have it any other way. Pets are our seat belts on the emotional roller coaster of life – they can be trusted, they keep us safe, and they sure do smooth out the ride.

cx

To Remember Me
Robert Test

Give **my sight** to the man who has never seen a sunrise,
a baby's face, or love in the eyes of a woman.
Give **my heart** to a person whose own heart has caused
nothing but endless days of pain.
Give **my blood** to the teenager who was pulled from
the wreckage of his car, so that he might live to see his
grandchildren play.
Give **my kidneys** to one who depends on a machine to
exist from week to week.
Take **my bones**, every muscle, every fibre and nerve in
my body and find a way to make a crippled child walk.
If you must bury something, let it be **my faults, my
weaknesses**, and all prejudice against my fellow man.
Give **my sins** to the devil.
Give **my soul** to God.
If, by chance, you wish **to remember me**, do it with a
kind deed or word to someone who needs you.
If you do all I have asked, I will live forever.

The Back Step
Lee Knowles

Every day at sunset
We watch the cows go by.
We always like to be there,
My grandmother and I.

They always go to water
Along the same old track,
But some must have a wander
And some go quickly back.

There's Mabel, Maude and Judy,
Mitzi who's always late
And Betsy Anne, who's rubbing
Her flanks against the gate.

Not for them the drabness
Of car or bike or train.
For them it's warming sunshine
And clear, refreshing rain.

It's giving milk each morning
And dozing in the grass.
It's never thinking over
How each new day will pass.

And we can share a little
In all this peace around,
Sitting on the back step
Scratching on the ground.

And so we dream together
And watch the cows go by,
While shelling peas and chatting –
My grandmother and I.

Helen the Badger
Molly Arbuthnott

Helen the badger was very house proud. She loved baking and had been looking after her home, Sunflower Sett, all her life. Her little patch of the Bluebell Wood was always spick and span. She spent her time cleaning and doing errands that other animals didn't have time to do, no job was ever too big or too boring for her and she never complained. She showered everything and everyone with love and, in return, everyone loved her.

One day, though, she didn't come out of her badger sett. She didn't come out the day after that or the day after that. The cobweb started getting grimy as Helen wasn't there to clean it with her duster, the bluebells started to wilt as Helen wasn't there to water them... All the animals were too busy with their own lives to notice, at first, but after a few days when there was still no sign of her, Fiona the owl began to get a bit worried. She flew around all the homes of the animals who lived in the Bluebell Wood and told them to go with her to Helen's house to see what was wrong.

So, on a sunny Sunday, all the bunnies, birds, squirrels, frogs and mice went to Helen's house to check she was OK. They knocked on the door... no reply. Harvey sneaked through a tiny hole by her door and... was inside. There, sitting on a corner of the sofa was Helen, sound asleep. "Poor Helen," Harvey thought to himself, "She has been so busy doing jobs for everyone else that she has worn herself out." Back outside Harvey announced, "I have an idea!" He explained to his assembled group that they should work together to give Helen the very biggest and best surprise. There was no time to lose! So, the dormice set to work washing their clothes and putting them on the line, helped by the birds. The hares and squirrels swept up all the leaves and the hedgehogs mopped the earth; the frogs dusted all the spiderwebs and watered and dusted the primroses and bluebells and the rabbits baked a tea fit for a princess.

Later that day, the animals assembled outside Helen's house and set the tea out outside in the lovely, clean area of the wood. Harvey sneaked through his little hole and carefully made a cup of tea for Helen.

He then left it beside her and started playing her piano very quietly. (He was a very good pianist) Helen, startled by the sound of the music, suddenly woke up and was very surprised to see Harvey inside her house

playing her piano. "What are you doing?" she asked.

"Doing something for you, for a change." Harvey replied. "Come with me," he said and led Helen towards her door and out of her house. The wood was looking more beautiful than she had ever seen it and there, sitting around a table laden with tea things, were all her friends. "Surprise!" they shouted. Helen started to cry with happiness! " They enjoyed a very jolly tea together. "From now on," Fiona said at the end, "we are going to work together and help each other." And so, all the animals in Bluebell Wood settled into a very happy routine living happily alongside each other and bringing brightness to each other's lives every day.

☃

While Waiting for Thee

Helen Steiner Rice

Don't weep at my grave,
For I am not there,
I've a date with a butterfly
To dance in the air.
I'll be singing in the sunshine,
Wild and free,
Playing tag with the wind,
While I'm waiting for thee.
The Comfort and Sweetness of Peace
After the clouds, the sunshine,
after the winter, the spring,
after the shower, the rainbow,
for life is a changeable thing.
After the night, the morning,
bidding all darkness cease,
after life's cares and sorrows,
the comfort and sweetness of peace.

I Cannot Go to School Today
Shel Silverstein - 1930-1999

"I cannot go to school today,"
Said little Peggy Ann McKay.
"I have the measles and the mumps,
A gash, a rash and purple bumps.
My mouth is wet, my throat is dry,
I'm going blind in my right eye.
My tonsils are as big as rocks,
I've counted sixteen chicken pox
And there's one more – that's seventeen,
And don't you think my face looks green?
My leg is cut – my eyes are blue –
It might be instamatic flu.
I cough and sneeze and gasp and choke,
I'm sure that my left leg is broke –
My hip hurts when I move my chin,
My belly button's caving in,
My back is wrenched, my ankle's sprained,
My 'pendix pains each time it rains.
My nose is cold, my toes are numb.
I have a sliver in my thumb.
My neck is stiff, my voice is weak,
I hardly whisper when I speak.
My tongue is filling up my mouth,
I think my hair is falling out.
My elbow's bent, my spine ain't straight,
My temperature is one-0-eight.
My brain is shrunk, I cannot hear,
There is a hole inside my ear.
I have a hangnail, and my heart is – what?
What's that? What's that you say?
You say today is ...Saturday?
G'bye, I'm going out to play!"

Heaven's Light *Anon*

The sun shines down upon us
and gives us warmth and light.
Then when the day has ended,
it disappears from sight.

Though we're left in darkness,
we know the sun has not died,
for it is shining brightly
on the world's other side.

So it is when one we love
comes to their end of days.
They just go to the other side
to shine their loving rays.

That's why heaven is a place
that glows beyond compare.
The lights of those who've left us
are all brightly shining there.

☙

The Farmer Stood at the Pearly Gates *Anon*

The farmer stood at the Pearly Gates,
His face was scarred and old,
He stood before the man of fate
To seek admission into the fold.
"What have you done" Saint Peter said,
"That you seek admission here?"
"I've been a farmer, Sir" he said,
"For many and many a year."
The Pearly Gates swung open wide
As Saint Peter pressed the bell,
"Come in" he said, "and choose your harp,
You've had your taste of Hell".

How Can The Sun Still Shine
Alex James

How can the sun still shine so brightly
birds sing and circle cloudless sky in flight
flowers bloom still fragrant as ever
and day still roll on gently in tonight.
How can this road that often we have driven
where folk still stand and chatter in the street
and children play
while my own grief unhidden
reflects in eyes of all those I meet.
How can the shopping precincts be so full
and television programmes be the same
and music on the airwaves keep on playing
and never once a mention of your name.
How can ordinary things that once I took for granted
continue on as though things are just the same
and everywhere your memory is planted
and every breath I take breathes out your name.
Take my arms for I no longer need them.
There is no one now I wish to hold
and taste and touch and sound will have no meaning
or summers warmth or winters icy cold.
Take away the laughter,
take those who still naive have life intact
take all the colour from the world it has no place here
for my own world is shrouded now in black.
Without you there's no reason for the sunshine.
No need to wrap up warm on starlit night.
Stand on a beach or watch a sunset.
My coloured world is changed
to black and white.
I wander round our old familiar places,
recalling you and how we used to be.
Around me just gaps and empty spaces.

And words that bring no comfort yet to me.
How can the sun still shine so brightly.
Birds sing and circle cloudless skies in flight.
Flowers bloom as fragrantly as ever.
and day still roll on gently in tonight.

☙

ONE GOOD THING ABOUT MUSIC, WHEN IT HITS YOU, YOU FEEL NO PAIN.

Bob Marley

☙

Oh dear, if you're reading this right now, I must have given up the ghost.
I hope you can forgive me for being
Such a stiff and unwelcoming host.
Just talk amongst yourself my friends, and share a toast or two.
For I am sure you will remember well
How I loved to drink with you.
Don't worry about mourning me, I was never easy to offend.
Feel free to share a story at my expense
And we'll have a good laugh at the end.
Kelly Roper

The Day was Passing me By
Florian Harrison

The day is passing me as a shadow;
The leaves rustle on the ground
and the rosy little boys
Half laughing at
the imagined dangers
Of a curly wee dog
leaping around their legs.

Was it in their eyes that I saw his,
Speckled green and brown
Or in their voice with hints of laugh
Or tears
Oh the day was but a shadow, passing me by.

Maybe it was in their heart
I could hear life growing step-by-step,
Oh little boys take the steps one-by-one
And slowly, inch-by-inch.
Don't wish to grow a beard,
Just play with the sand and build
castles in the air.
Your birthright is the world
The world has open doors for the ones
who want in. Walk slowly and let the light
flicker, till at noon it shines bright.
Till you know to receive and to give.

The day was passing me by like the shadow
Of a soul.

❧

A Clothesline Poem
Marilyn Walker

A clothesline was a news forecast, to neighbours passing by.
There were no secrets you could keep, when clothes were hung to dry.

It also was a friendly link, for neighbours always knew,
If company had stopped on by, to spend a night or two.

For then you'd see the fancy sheets and towels upon the line;
You'd see the company tablecloths, with intricate design.

The line announced a baby's birth, to folks who lived inside,
As brand new infant clothes, were hung so carefully with pride.

The ages of the children, could so readily be known
By watching how the sizes changed, you'd know how much they'd grown.

It also told when illness struck, as extra sheets were hung;
Then nightclothes, and a bathrobe too, haphazardly were strung.

It also said "On holiday", when lines hung limp and bare.
It told "We're back!" when full lines sagged, with not an inch to spare.

New folks in town were scorned upon, if washing was dingy grey,
As neighbours carefully raised their brows, and looked disgustedly away.

But clotheslines now are of the past, for dryers make work much less,
Now what goes on inside a home, is anybody's guess.

I really miss that way of life; it was a friendly sign,
When neighbours knew each other best, by what was hanging on the line.

☙

Death is a Funny Thing
Joe Brainard

Death is a funny thing. Most people are afraid of it, and yet they don't even know what it is.

Perhaps we can clear this up.

What is death?

Death is it. That's it. Finished. "Finito." Over and out. No more.

Death is many different things to many different people. I think it is safe to say, however, that most people don't like it.

Why?

Because they are afraid of it.

Why are they afraid of it?

Because they don't understand it.

I think that the best way to try to understand death is to think about it a lot. Try to come to terms with it. Try to really understand it. Give it a chance!

Sometimes it helps if we try to visualise things.

Try to visualise, for example, someone sneaking up behind your back and hitting you over the head with a giant hammer.

Some people prefer to think of death as a more spiritual thing. Where the soul somehow separates itself from the mess and goes on living forever somewhere else. Heaven and hell being the most traditional choices.

Death has a very black reputation but, actually, to die is a perfectly normal thing to do.

And it's so wholesome: being a very important part of nature's big picture. Trees die, don't they? And flowers?

I think it's always nice to know that you are not alone. Even in death.

Let's think about ants for a minute. Millions of ants die every day, and do we care? No. And I'm sure that ants feel the same way about us.

But suppose – just suppose – that we didn't have to die.

That wouldn't be so great either. If a 90-year-old man can hardly stand up, can you imagine what it would be like to be 500 years old?

Another comforting thought about death is that 80 years or so after you die nobody who knew you will still be alive to miss you.

And after you're dead, you won't even know it.

We're Flying with the Eagles Now
Anon

We're flying with the eagles now
We've just begun our sail
We've got our mission all mapped out
It will be a wondrous tale
We'll land on every foreign shore
Though we've not long to stay...
We're headed toward
The rainbow's end
Where the sun is shining...
Flying with the eagles now
And we must be on our way...

Up here we're free from all troubles
Up here it seems that life's all so clear
As we're in flight and we glide
Into the dark still night...
Look now the stars are appearing
So close we almost can touch
Their soft glistening eyes
They are angels in disguise

℃ℬ

YOU THINK DOGS WILL NOT BE IN HEAVEN? I TELL YOU, THEY WILL BE THERE LONG BEFORE ANY OF US

Robert Louis Stevenson

Little Boy Blue
Eugene Field

The little toy dog is covered with dust,
But sturdy and stanch he stands;
And the little toy soldier is red with rust,
And his musket moulds in his hands.
Time was when the little toy dog was new,
And the soldier was passing fair;
And that was the time when our Little Boy Blue
Kissed them and put them there.

"Now, don't you go till I come," he said,
"And don't you make any noise!"
So, toddling off to his trundle-bed,
He dreamt of the pretty toys;
And, as he was dreaming, an angel song
Awakened our Little Boy Blue –
Oh! the years are many, the years are long,
But the little toy friends are true!

Ay, faithful to Little Boy Blue they stand,
Each in the same old place –
Awaiting the touch of a little hand,
The smile of a little face;
And they wonder, as waiting the long years through
In the dust of that little chair,
What has become of our Little Boy Blue,
Since he kissed them and put them there.

☙

The tree I had in the garden as a child, my beech tree,
I used to climb up there and spend hours. I took my
homework up there, my books, I went up there if I was
sad, and it just felt very good to be up there among the
green leaves and the birds and the sky. *Jane Goodall*

And above all,
watch with glittering eyes the whole world around you
because the greatest secrets are always
hidden in the most unlikely places.
Those who don't believe in magic will never find it.

Roald Dahl

☙

These are my Footprints
from Divine Fancies, 1632

These are my footprints, so perfect and so small.
These tiny footprints, never touched the ground at all.
Not one tiny footprint, for now I have my wings.
These tiny footprints were meant for other things.
You will hear my tiny footprints, in the patter of the rain.
Gentle drops like angels tears, of joy and not from pain.
You will see my tiny footprints, in each butterflies' lazy dance.
I'll let you know I'm with you, if you give me just a chance.
You will see my tiny footprints, in the rustle of the leaves.
I will whisper names into the wind, and call each one that grieves.
Most of all, these tiny footprints, are found in Mummy's heart,
'cause even though I'm gone now, we'll never truly part."

☙

IN A GENTLE WAY, YOU CAN SHAKE THE WORLD *Mahatma Gandi*

Buying a Miracle

A little girl went to her bedroom and pulled a glass jelly jar from its hiding place in the closet. She poured the change out on the floor and counted it carefully. Three times, even. The total had to be exactly perfect. No chance here for mistakes. Carefully placing the coins back in the jar and twisting on the cap, she slipped out the back door and made her way to the pharmacy. She waited patiently for the pharmacist to give her some attention, but he was too busy at this moment. Tess twisted her feet to make a scuffing noise. Nothing. She cleared her throat with the most disgusting sound she could muster. No good. Finally she took a shilling from her jar and banged it on the glass counter. That did it! 'And what do you want?' the pharmacist asked in an annoyed tone of voice. I'm talking to my brother from Chicago whom I haven't seen in ages,' he said without waiting for a reply to his question. 'Well, I want to talk to you about my brother,' Tess answered back in the same annoyed tone. 'He's really, really sick....and I want to buy a miracle.' 'I beg your pardon?' said the pharmacist. 'His name is Andrew and he has something bad growing inside his head and my Daddy says only a miracle can save him now. So how much does a miracle cost?' 'We don't sell miracles here, little girl. I'm sorry but I can't help you,' the pharmacist said, softening a little. 'Listen, I have the money to pay for it. If it isn't enough, I will get the rest. Just tell me how much it costs.' The pharmacist's brother was a well dressed man. He stooped down and asked the little girl, 'What kind of a miracle does your brother need?' ' I don't know,' Tess replied with her eyes welling up. I just know he's really sick and Mummy says he needs an operation. But my Daddy can't pay for it, so I want to use my money.' 'How much do you have?' asked the man from Chicago . 'One pound and eleven pence,' Tess answered barely audible. 'And it's all the money I have, but I can get some more if I need to.' 'Well, what a coincidence,' smiled the man. 'A pound and eleven pence – the exact price of a miracle for little brothers.' He took her money in one hand and with the other hand he grasped her mitten and said 'Take me to where you live. I want to see your brother and meet your parents. Let's see if I have the miracle you need.' That well-dressed man was Dr. Carlton Armstrong, a surgeon, specialising in neurosurgery. The operation was completed free of charge and it wasn't long until Andrew was home again

and doing well. Mum and Dad were happily talking about the chain of events that had led them to this place. 'That surgery,' her Mum whispered. 'was a real miracle.. I wonder how much it would have cost?' Tess smiled. She knew exactly how much a miracle cost... one dollar and eleven cents... plus the faith of a little child. In our lives, we never know how many miracles we will need. A miracle is not the suspension of natural law, but the operation of a higher law.

ॐ

The Parting Glass

Oh all the time that e'er I spent,
I spent it in good company;
And any harm that e'er I've done,
I trust it was to none but me;
May those I've loved through all the years
Have memories now they'll e'er recall;
So fill me to the parting glass,
Goodnight, and joy be with you all.
Oh all the comrades that e'er I had,
Are sorry for my going away;
And all the loved ones that e'er I had
Would wish me one more day to stay.
But since it falls unto my lot
That I should leave and you should not,
I'll gently rise and I'll softly call
Goodnight, and joy be with you all.
Of all good times that e'er we shared,
I leave to you fond memory;
And for all the friendship that e'er we had
I ask you to remember me;
And when you sit and stories tell,
I'll be with you and help recall;
So fill to me the parting glass,
God bless, and joy be with you all.

Pennies from Heaven

Anon

I found a penny today
Just laying on the ground.
But it's not just a penny
This little coin I've found.

Found pennies come from heaven
that's what my Grandpa told me.
He said Angels tossed them down
Oh, how I loved that story!

He said when an Angel misses you
They toss a penny down,
sometimes just to cheer you up
To make a smile out of your frown.

So don't pass by that penny
When you're feeling blue.
It may be a penny from heaven
That an Angel's tossed to you.

☙

PEOPLE MAY FORGET WHAT YOU SAID OR WHAT YOU DID, BUT WILL NEVER FORGET HOW YOU MADE THEM FEEL

i carry your heart with me

e e Cummings

i carry your heart with me *(i carry it in*
my heart) i am never without it *(anywhere*
i go you go, my dear; and whatever is done
by only me is your doing, my darling)
i fear
no fate *(for you are my fate, my sweet)* i want
no world *(for beautiful you are my world, my true)*
and it's you are whatever a moon has always meant
and whatever a sun will always sing is you

here is the deepest secret nobody knows
(here is the root of the root and the bud of the bud
and the sky of the sky of a tree called life; which grows
higher than soul can hope or mind can hide)
and this is the wonder that's keeping the stars apart

i carry your heart *(i carry it in my heart)*

You have no enemies, you say?

Charles Mackay

You have no enemies, you say?
Alas! my friend, the boast is poor;
He who has mingled in the fray
Of duty, that the brave endure,
Must have made foes! If you have none,
Small is the work that you have done.
You've hit no traitor on the hip,
You've dashed no cup from perjured lip,
You've never turned the wrong to right,
You've been a coward in the fight.

The Sandpiper

The Seven Wonders of the World

A group of American school children were asked to list what they thought were the present "Seven Wonders of the World." Though there were some disagreements, the following received the most votes:

1. *Egypt's Great Pyramids*
2. *Taj Mahal*
3. *Grand Canyon*
4. *Panama Canal*
5. *Empire State Building*
6. *St. Peter's Basilica*
7. *Great Wall of China*

While gathering the votes, the teacher noted that one student had not finished her paper yet. So she asked the girl if she was having trouble with her list. The little girl replied, "Yes, a little. I couldn't quite make up my mind because there are so many." The teacher said, "Well, tell us what you have, and maybe we can help." The girl hesitated, then read, "I think the "Seven Wonders of the World" are:

1. *To see*
2. *To hear*
3. *To touch*
4. *To taste*
5. *To feel*
6. *To laugh*
7. *To love*

The room was so quiet you could hear a pin drop.
The things we overlook as simple and ordinary and that we take for granted are truly wondrous. A gentle reminder – that the most precious things in life cannot be built by hand or bought by man.

"Just living is not enough," said the butterfly, "one must have sunshine, freedom and a little flower."

Hans Christian Anderson

Grumpy Grandad

"No jumping in puddles" I heard him say
Walking along with his Grandad today
"Spoilsport" I nearly cried out, but maybe he would
Turn and give me a clout
Think of the joy he denied him today
A joy I remember to this very day.
The next puddle I see I will jump in with glee
In two weeks' time I will be 83.

Succession
N.E.W. Ireland 2021

Now grey at the temples, lines around my old eyes,
Time catches us all, a fact we cannot disguise.
And now the young of the parish, we lead by the hand,
And impart on them knowledge, to look after this land.

> **The countryside is a book, from which we all learn,**
> **Each day is a page, we are willing to turn.**
> **Four chapters in all, much joy they will bring.**
> **Named summer and autumn, winter and spring.**

Through the eyes of the young, sometimes things look the same,
We need to take care, and find time to explain.
To point out the difference, in what we see every day,
Like the nest of a magpie and a red squirrels drey.

> **Showing the young, who are eager to know,**
> **The contrast in flight, between a rook and a crow.**
> **And that glimpse of grey bird, which we saw on our walk,**
> **Was it the cuckoo of spring, or a sleek sparrow hawk?**

Show them the flowers, appearing when the sun shines,
The bright dandelion, the shy celandine.
Now listen quietly, what can you hear,
Is it the cry of the vixen, or the small muntjac deer?

> **Tread soft on the heather, when red stags you observe,**
> **Sometimes we cull, sometimes we conserve.**
> **The jay in the hedgerow, what is it he mocks,**
> **The farm cat out prowling or the lurking red fox?**

Take the time to sit down, and watch for a while,
Observe country life, from an old wooden style.
Every meadow you walk through, on hill, dale or fell,
Has a myth or a legend, or a story to tell.

Life in the country, is a joy to behold,
With a moon made of silver, and sunsets of gold.
The keys to its secrets, are just held by the few,
We pass them on wisely, and toast them with dew.

☙

When a light is as bright
Donna Ashworth

When a light is as bright
as the light you shone
there's no such thing
as truly gone

When a smile is as precious
As the one you wore
You nestle in hearts
Forevermore

When one so loved
is taken too soon
the love that is left
could outshine the moon

So much love with no place
to be truly at peace
so we love you more
bittersweet release

Sweet child
You were here
For so little time
But the hole that you left

Grows ever wide.

The Sandpiper

Dear Nana, how we'll miss you
James Burnett of Leys

Dear Nana how we'll miss you, on this we all agree;
That's from all your little ones and especially from me.
And also from our parents, when away they always knew
That we were in the safest hands, so from all of us, thank you.

>**Dear Nana how we'll miss you**, thanks for all you've done for us;
>Cooking, washing, ironing, sewing; and never any fuss.
>Of all the Nanas in this world, you are certainly the best;
>You led us through our early years and when we left the nest.

Dear Nana how we'll miss you and for you we will long;
You helped us all to read and write and learn what's right and wrong;
Football, darts or snooker may not have come from you;
But the way in which we fill our lives, credit's where it's due.

>**Dear Nana how we'll miss you**, how would we have fared alone;
>All the stress and care and work and no complaint or moan;
>To you we owe such gratitude and that we say sincerely;
>You never said an unkind word, we love you very dearly.

Dear Nana how we'll miss you; for you our lives were brighter;
In that garden where you're now at rest, life will be a little lighter;
We knew that you were suffering, but never were conceding;
But doubtless you'll be picking flowers, or on your knees and weeding

ᛦ

"THE DREAM BEGINS, MOST OF THE TIME,
WITH A TEACHER WHO BELIEVES IN YOU,
WHO TUGS AND PUSHES AND LEADS YOU
TO THE NEXT PLATEAU, SOMETIMES WITH
A SHARP STICK CALLED TRUTH."
Dan Rathe

When I Think Of Death
Maya Angelou

When I think of death, and of late the idea has come with alarming
frequency, I seem at peace with the idea that a day will dawn when I will
no longer be among those living in this valley of strange humours.
I can accept the idea of my own demise, but I am unable to accept the
death of anyone else. I find it impossible to let a friend or relative go into
that country of no return. Disbelief becomes my close companion, and
anger follows in its wake. I answer the heroic question 'Death, where is thy
sting?' with ' it's here in my heart and mind and memories.'

ᥩ

Today was a Difficult Day
AA Milne

"Today was a Difficult Day," said Pooh.
There was a pause.
"Do you want to talk about it?" asked Piglet.
"No," said Pooh after a bit. "No, I don't think I do."
"That's okay," said Piglet, and he came and sat
beside his friend.
"What are you doing?" asked Pooh.
"Nothing, really," said Piglet. "Only, I know what
Difficult Days are like. I quite often don't feel like
talking about it on my Difficult Days either.
"But goodness," continued Piglet, "Difficult Days
are so much easier when you know you've got
someone there for you. And I'll always be here for
you, Pooh."
And as Pooh sat there, working through in his head
his Difficult Day, while the solid, reliable Piglet sat
next to him quietly, swinging his little legs…
he thought that his best friend had never been
more right.

Catch A Rainbow
Brian Whittingham

If I could catch a Rainbow

I'd hang it round your shoulders.
A rainbow scarf.
It's pot of gold
next to the beat of your heart.

If I could catch a Rainbow

I'd make
rainbow puddles.
For you to splash colour
wherever your steps may take you.

If I could catch a Rainbow

I'd turn it upside down.
A rainbow rocking bed
to let you float to a land of bliss,
drift safe on dozing dreams.

If I could catch a Rainbow

CB

*Just like the butterfly,
I too will awaken in my own time.*

Deborah Chaskin

There's an Elephant in the Room

There's an elephant in the room.
It is large and squatting, so it is hard to get around it.
Yet we squeeze by with, "How are you?" and "I'm fine,"
and a thousand other forms of trivial chatter.
We talk about the weather. We talk about work.
We talk about everything else, except the elephant in the room.

There's an elephant in the room.
We all know it's there. We are thinking about the elephant
as we talk together. It is constantly on our minds.
For, you see, it is a very large elephant.
It has hurt us all.
But we don't talk about the elephant.

Oh, please, let's talk about the elephant in the room.
For if I cannot, then you are leaving me... alone... in a room...
with an elephant.

❧

The Toadstool House

I wish I lived in a toadstool house,
Beneath an old Oak tree,
With a tiny door and a chimney pot,
And windows – one, two, three.
I'd play with each wee squirrel,
Who chanced to come my way,
I'd get to know the woodland birds,
And feed them every day.
And if you'd ever wandered by,
I'd ask you in to tea,
Inside my little toadstool house,
Beneath the old Oak Tree.

The Sandpiper

God's Garden
Anon

God looked around his garden
And found an empty place,
He then looked down upon the earth
And saw your tired face.
He put his arms around you
And lifted you to rest.
God's garden must be beautiful
He always takes the best.
He knew that you were suffering
He knew you were in pain.
He knew that you would never
Get well on earth again.
He saw the road was getting rough
And the hills were hard to climb.
So he closed your weary eyelids
And whispered, 'Peace be thine'.
It broke our hearts to lose you
But you didn't go alone,
For part of us went with you
The day God called you home.

ॐ

"And when your sorrow is comforted (time soothes all
sorrows) you will be content that you have known me.
You will always be my friend. You will want to laugh
with me. And you will sometimes open your window,
so, for that pleasure …And your friends will be properly
astonished to see you laughing as you look up at the sky!
Then you will say to them, 'Yes, the stars always make me
laugh!' And they will think you are crazy. It will be a very
shabby trick that I shall have played on you…"

Antoine de Saint-Exupery, The Little Prince

In 1918 Dorothy Burnett (sister to Arthur, the 8th Laird of Kemnay) wrote a
poem describing the perfect country garden that many city dwellers would
have dreamed of at the end of the First World War.
The garden at Kemnay still has much in common with this description
(including the rather haphazard planting scheme) so the verse continually
comes to mind when pruning the roses, collecting the gooseberries or seeing
the delphiniums bloom:

We shall have a garden with cherry trees in May;
The path shall be of flagstones and alternate all the way
A gooseberry and rose bush; there must be Bergamot
And all the sweet old-fashioned flowers not one must be forgot.
There will be a grey wall, six feet high or so,
Every rose that rambles we'll plant and watch it grow,
All the little rock things will creep along the top,
Silvery clumps of saxifrage and yellow golden crop.
We shall have a border close against the wall,
Blue delphiniums at the back and annuals through it all;
but we won't be so modern as to have a colour scheme,
We'd rather have all the colours in this garden of our dream,
Then just beneath the window, where the night wind can blow,
We'll have a bed of all the very sweetest things that grow.
Scented stock and mignonette with every kind of thyme,
'Tis the very perfect paradise, this garden dream of mine.
I can see my garden now, just turn towards the west,
Half close your eyes, remember, and I think God does the rest.
"Houses and smoke", you only see a dirty London Square,
My friend, it's plain you don't possess a garden in the air.

Dorothy Burnett (1918)

Not for Me a Young Man's Death
Roger McGough

Not for me a young man's death
Not a car crash, whiplash
John Doe, DOA at A&E kind of death.
Not a gun in hand, in a far off land
IED at the roadside death

Not a slow-fade, razor blade
bloodbath in the bath, death.
Jump under a train, Kurt Cobain
bullet in the brain, death

Not a horse-riding paragliding
mountain climbing fall, death.
Motorcycle into an old stone wall
you know the kind of death, death

My nights are rarely unruly. My days
of all night parties are over, well and truly.
No mistresses no red sports cars
no shady deals no gangland bars
no drugs no fags no rock'n'roll
Time alone has taken its toll

Not for me a young man's death
Not a domestic brawl, blood in the hall
knife in the chest, death.
Not a drunken binge, dirty syringe
"What a waste of a life" death.

ॐ

You Think you can Defy Me
Erin Hanson

You think you can defy me,
That I'm a tick in just one box,
Like my being is a door,
That a single key unlocks,
But let me tell you something,
I have the universe inside,
I hold an untamed ocean
With a constant changing tide,
I'm home to endless mountains,
With tips that touch the sky,
Flocks of grand migrating birds,
And deserts harsh and dry,
I house the wildest rivers,
And a host of sweeping plains,
I feel in waves of sunshine,
Or in unrelenting rains,
Don't tell me that you know me,
That "this right here is what you are",
I am the universe in motion,
For I was born from the stars.

☙

LET US REMEMBER:
ONE BOOK, ONE PEN,
ONE CHILD
AND ONE TEACHER
CAN CHANGE THE WORLD.

Malala

When God Sent You to Help Me Heal
Anon

When God sent you to help me heal
He sent a special gift.
It was you, a gentle carer
That he would bless me with.

A carer that would laugh with me,
A carer that would cry.
A carer that would pick me up
And lift my spirits high

A carer with a great big smile
And an even bigger heart
A carer with such gentle ways
Who cared right from the start.

A trusty nurse – you truly are.
You stand above the rest
And all of those you care for;
With you – they are truly blessed.

ॐ

Here's to the Crazy Ones   *Steve Jobs*

Here's to the crazy ones. The misfits. The rebels. The troublemakers.
The round pegs in the square holes. The ones who see things differently.
They're not fond of rules. And they have no respect for the status quo.
You can quote them, disagree with them, glorify or vilify them. About
the only thing you can't do is ignore them. Because they change things.
They push the human race forward. And while some may see them as
the crazy ones, we see genius. Because the people who are crazy enough
to think they can change the world, are the ones who do.

What Is It?
R J Heaney

Love is peace
Love is pleasure
Love is sorrow
Measure for measure

Love is parting
Love is joining
Love is madness
Passion boiling

Love is nineteen
Love is wonderful
Love is twenty three
Even more plentiful

Love is growing
Love is caring
Love is wanting
Love is sharing

Love is birthdays
Love is all days
Especially today
I love you always

Love today
Love tomorrow
Smile and be happy
And your thoughts I'll borrow

Love is doing
Love is loving
Tender thoughts
I send my darling.

The Sandpiper

A Boy and His Dog
Edgar Guest

A boy and his dog make a glorious pair:
No better friendship is found anywhere,
For they talk and they walk and they run and they play,
And they have their deep secrets for many a day;
And that boy has a comrade who thinks and who feels,
Who walks down the road with a dog at his heels.

> He may go where he will and his dog will be there,
> May revel in mud and his dog will not care;
> Faithful he'll stay for the slightest command
> And bark with delight at the touch of his hand;
> Oh, he owns a treasure which nobody steals,
> Who walks down the road with a dog at his heels.

No other can lure him away from his side;
He's proof against riches and station and pride;
Fine dress does not charm him, and flattery's breath
Is lost on the dog, for he's faithful to death;
He sees the great soul which the body conceals –
Oh, it's great to be young with a dog at your heels!

☙

A Candle, A Candle
Anon

A candle, a candle, to light me to bed;
A pillow, a pillow to tuck up my head.
The moon is as sleepy as sleepy can be,
The stars are all pointing their fingers at me,
And Missus Hop-Robin, way up in her nest,
Is rocking her tired little babies to rest.
So give me a blanket to tuck up my toes,
And a little soft pillow to snuggle my nose

How do You Like to Go Up in a Swing
Robert Louis Stevenson

How do you like to go up in a swing,
    Up in the air so blue?
Oh, I do think it the pleasantest thing
    Ever a child can do!

Up in the air and over the wall,
    Till I can see so wide,
Rivers and trees and cattle and all
    Over the countryside –

Till I look down on the garden green,
    Down on the roof so brown –
Up in the air I go flying again,
    Up in the air and down!

ᘓ

An Irishman's Philosophy

There are only two things to worry about:
    Either you are well or you are sick.

If you are sick,
Then there are only two things to worry about:
    Either you will get well or you will die.

If you get well,
Then there are only two things to worry about:
    Either you will go to heaven or hell.

If you go to heaven, there is nothing to worry about.

But if you go to hell,
You'll be so damn busy shaking hands with friends
    You won't have time to worry!

Up-Hill
Christina Rossetti

Does the road wind up-hill all the way?
    Yes, to the very end.
Will the day's journey take the whole long day?
    From morn to night, my friend.

But is there for the night a resting-place?
    A roof for when the slow dark hours begin.
May not the darkness hide it from my face?
    You cannot miss that inn.

Shall I meet other wayfarers at night?
    Those who have gone before.
Then must I knock, or call when just in sight?
    They will not keep you standing at that door.

Shall I find comfort, travel-sore and weak?
    Of labour you shall find the sum.
Will there be beds for me and all who seek?
    Yea, beds for all who come.

☙

Rise up this mornin'
Smile with the risin' sun
Three little birds
Pitched by my doorstep
Singin' sweet songs
Of melodies pure and true
Sayin', "This is my message to you, whoo-hoo"
Singin', don't worry, about a thing
'Cause every little thing, is gonna be all right'

Bob Marley

Sun and Moon
Nadia McGhee

I once met the sun
And she was very bright
She always talked
She was a huge ball of light
She told me about the things
She sees throughout the day
And when I thought she was done talking
She suddenly had more to say
And when she left at dusk
I did not feel completely whole
And I realised all of her talking
Did nothing for my soul

I once met the moon
And she was very calm
She looked at me as if she knew the secrets
That I held in my palm
She did not speak once
The silence brought me peace
It was as if her silence
Was fixing me piece by piece
And when she left at dawn
I felt something deep within me
And I knew that her silence
Had set my soul free.

CB

Look to the stars and from them learn

Albert Einstein

Questions At Night
Louis Untermeyer

Why
Is the sky?
What starts the thunder overhead?
Who makes the crashing noise?
Are the angels falling out of bed?
Are they breaking all their toys?

Why does the sun go down so soon?
Why do the night-clouds crawl
Hungrily up to the new-laid moon
And swallow it, shell and all?

If there's a Bear among the stars,
As all the people say,
Won't he jump over those Pasture-bars
And drink up the Milky Way?

Does every star that happens to fall
Turn into a fire-fly?
Can't it ever get back to Heaven at all?
And why
Is the sky?

 C3

" If one feels the need of something grand, something
infinite, something that makes one feel aware of
God, one need not go far to find it. I think that I see
something deeper, more infinite, more eternal than
the ocean in the expression of the eyes of a little baby
when it wakes in the morning and coos or laughs
because it sees the sun shining on its cradle."

Vincent van Gogh

A Little House
Elizabeth Godley

In a great big wood in a great big tree,
there's the nicest little house that could possibly be.
There's a tiny little knocker on the tiny little door,
and a tiny little carpet on the tiny little floor.
There's a tiny little table, and a tiny little bed,
and a tiny little pillow for a tiny weeny head;
A tiny little blanket, and a tiny little sheet,
and a tiny water bottle (hot) for tiny little feet.
A tiny little eiderdown; a tiny little chair;
and a tiny little kettle for the owner (when he's there.)
In a tiny little larder there's a tiny thermos bottle
for a tiny little greedy man who knows the Woods Of Pottle
There's a tiny little peg for a tiny little hat
and a tiny little dog and a tiny little cat.

If you've got a little house and you keep it spic and span,
Perhaps there'll come to live in it a tiny little man
You may not ever see him, he is extremely shy;
But if you find a crumpled sheet –
Or pins upon the window seat –
Or see the marks of tiny feet –
You'll know the reason why.

ప

Death.
One who died is only a little way ahead of procession all moving that way. When we round the corner we will see him again. We have only lost him for a moment because we fell behind, stopping to tie a shoelace.

J.M. Barrie

The Sandpiper

The Rainbow
Christina Rossetti

Boats sail on the rivers,
And ships sail on the seas;
But clouds that sail across the sky
Are prettier far than these.

There are bridges on the rivers,
As pretty as you please;
But the bow that bridges heaven,
And overtops the trees,
And builds a road from earth to sky,
Is prettier far than these.

∝

Smiling Is Infectious
Spike Milligan

Smiling is infectious,
you catch it like the flu,
When someone smiled at me today,
I started smiling too.
I passed around the corner
and someone saw my grin.
When he smiled I realised
I'd passed it on to him.
I thought about that smile,
then thought about its worth.
A single smile, just like mine
could travel round the earth.
So, if you feel a smile begin,
don't leave it undetected.
Let's start an epidemic quick,
and get the world infected!

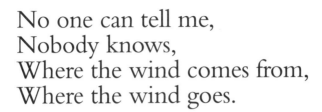

No one can tell me,
Nobody knows,
Where the wind comes from,
Where the wind goes.

It's flying from somewhere
As fast as it can,
I couldn't keep up with it,
Not if I ran.

But if I stopped holding
The string of my kite,
It would blow with the wind
For a day and a night.

And then when I found it,
Wherever it blew,
I should know that the wind
Had been going there too.

So then I could tell them
Where the wind goes...
But where the wind comes from
Nobody knows.

A.A. Milne

The Sandpiper

All in a Day's Work
KJ paramedic Aberdeen

So, I was on nightshift based at Kincorth. Felt peckish so headed down to the local supermarket to buy a packet of custard creams.

On the way back I crossed over George VI bridge where I saw a woman perched on the parapet crying and yelling that she was going to jump. I stopped the car and blocked lane one of the bridge to provide a safe area and asked for police assistance.

On climbing back out of the car the woman yelled that if she saw or heard a police car then she would definitely jump.

Just by chatting to her I was able to calm her down a bit and turned my back on her to quickly and quietly ask for an unmarked police car to attend.

I looked over the bridge and saw that the tide was in so the river was high. Meanwhile the woman was listening to an Adele song on repeat. After listening to "Someone like you" for what seemed like an eternity, I was tempted to jump myself!

I asked her if I could put a blanket over shoulders to warm her up and she started screaming again and broke down. I chose this moment to offer her a custard cream. She froze for a second, taken aback by the fact that she was threatening to take her own life, and I was offering her a custard cream. As she glanced at the custard cream, I laid the blanket around her and decided that it was now or never to pull her to safety. Thankfully it was a success but she was not happy, even after being offered a custard cream. Police arrived soon after and I returned to base for a much needed cuppa and a packet of custard creams, relieved that the woman would hopefully go on to receive the care she needed to make herself better.

I think of her every time I am offered a custard cream!

Piglet Let Himself into Pooh's House...
A.A. Milne

Piglet let himself into Pooh's house to find his friend lying on the floor under his kitchen table with a blanket over his head.

"Um... Pooh? What are you doing?"

"Hiding," muttered Pooh.

"Hiding from what?"

"Everything," said Pooh with a heavy sigh. "Listen, I know we were meant to be going out with Rabbit and Tigger for a few drinks tonight, but I just don't think I can face leaving the house today. You go without me. I'll be Absolutely Fine."

Piglet stood for a moment, looking at the blanketed mound of his friend underneath the table. Then, carefully, he took off his shoes, lowered himself down onto the floor, crawled underneath the table and put his head underneath the blanket next to a surprised looking Pooh.

"What are you doing?" asked Pooh.

"I'm just being here," said Piglet. "With you."

"But I'm Absolutely Fine," said Pooh. "You go out and have fun. I'll be Absolutely Fine."

"No," said Piglet. "All things considered, I don't think that I will go out. I think that, actually, I'm going to stay right here with you, under the table, with our heads underneath a blanket. Because what I have learnt, over my many years, is that the people who say that they're Absolutely Fine... actually are quite often the people who need a good friend with them most of all."

Pooh gulped, and found that he couldn't actually speak, but he nodded his head so vigorously that he nearly dislodged the blanket from atop them, and Piglet understood completely.

enduring. do not underestimate

someone who has lost everything and is still here to tell the story. do not underestimate someone who has fought dearly for sobriety. peace. forgiveness. self-love. freedom. authenticity. truth. do not underestimate the lonely. they have braved wars that only those who understand the absence of human connection, can do. even now, they are holding it all together while coming so wildly undone. and sometimes we may see them unravel ever so softly. or loudly. or however their soul unties its cage the best. do not underestimate the ones who have suffered the kind of grief that does not seem to end. who have been broken in places you did not even know existed. the ones who fell into silence because their lungs had no words left to speak. we will not always be strong. no. but we are enduring.

ullie-kaye

The Little Boy And The Old Man
Shel Silverstein

Said the little boy, sometimes I drop my spoon.
Said the little old man, I do that too.
The little boy whispered, I wet my pants.
I do too, laughed the old man.
Said the little boy, I often cry.
The old man nodded. So do I.
But worst of all, said the boy,
it seems grown-ups don't pay attention to me.
And he felt the warmth of a wrinkled old hand.
I know what you mean, said the little old man.

℃

*We pass this way but once
let's live each day as richly as we can
with the people we love
doing the things
that matter most*

The Robin

resilience

ɞ

There is no despair so absolute as that which comes
with the first moments of our first great sorrow,
when we have not yet known what it is to have suffered
and be healed, to have despaired and have recovered hope.

George Eliot

White Noise
Barbara Vance

In all the world
There's nothing like
The sound of falling snow –

The only noise
I've ever known
That makes the clocks move slow;

The only sound
That sweeps away
The din of city streets;

And wraps around,
In soft embrace,
'Most everyone it meets;

A sound that's not
A sound at all –
A quiet, soft and dear,

That comforts all
The sleepy souls
Who sit, and watch, and hear.

ೞ

*Tomorrow will be a good day
My today was alright and my tomorrow will be better
that's the way I've always looked at life
The sun will shine on you again and the clouds will go away*

Captain Tom

10 Commandments from a Dog's Point of View
Stan Rawlinson

1. My life is likely to last 10 to 15 years; any separation from you will be painful for me. Remember that before you adopt me.

2. Give me time to understand what you want from me; don't be impatient, short-tempered, or irritable.

3. Place your trust in me and I will always trust you back. Respect is earned not given as an inalienable right.

4. Don't be angry with me for long and don't lock me up as punishment; I am not capable of understanding why. I only know I have been rejected. You have your work, entertainment, and friends – I only have you.

5. Talk to me. Even if I don't understand your words, I do understand your voice and your tone. You only have to look at my tail.

6. Be aware that however you treat me, I'll never forget it, and if it's cruel, it may affect me forever.

7. Please don't hit me. I can't hit back, but I can bite and scratch, and I really don't ever want to do that

8. Before you scold me for being uncooperative, obstinate, or lazy, ask yourself if something might be bothering me. Perhaps I'm not getting the right foods or I've been out in the sun too long, or my heart is getting old and weak. It may be I am just dog-tired.

9. Take care of me when I get old. You too will grow old and may also need love, care, comfort, and attention.

10. Go with me on difficult journeys. Never say, "I can't bear to watch" or "Let it happen in my absence." Everything is easier for me if you are there. Remember, regardless of what you do, I will always love you.

Grief is Like Carrying a Stone in Your Pocket
Jessica Watson

"The best way I can describe grief as the years go by is to say it's similar to carrying a stone in your pocket.

When you walk, the stone brushes against your skin. You feel it. You always feel it. But depending on the way you stand or the way your body moves, the smooth edges might barely graze your body.

Sometimes you lean the wrong way or you turn too quickly and a sharp edge pokes you. Your eyes water and you rub your wound but you have to keep going because not everyone knows about your stone, or if they do, they don't realize it can still bring this much pain.

There are days you are simply happy now, smiling comes easy and you laugh without thinking. You slap your leg during that laughter and you feel your stone and aren't sure whether you should be laughing still. The stone still hurts.

Once in a while you can't take your hand off that stone. You run it over your fingers and roll it in your palm and are so preoccupied by its weight, you forget things like your car keys and home address. You try to leave it alone but you just can't. You want to take a nap but it's been so many years since you've called in "sad" you're not sure anyone would understand anymore or if they ever did.

But most days you can take your hand in and out of your pocket, feel your stone and even smile at its unwavering presence. You've accepted this stone as your own, crossing your hands over it, saying "mine" as children do.

You rest more peacefully than you once did, you've learned to move forward the best you can. Some days you want to show the world what a beautiful memory you're holding. But most days you twirl it through your fingers, smile and look to the sky. You squeeze your hands together and hope you are living in a way that honors the missing piece you carry, until your arms are full again."

My dear,

In the midst of HATE, I found there was, within me, an invincible love.
In the midst of TEARS, I found there was, within me, an invincible smile.
In the midst of CHAOS, I found there was, within me, an invincible calm.
I realised, through it all, that…
In the midst of WINTER, I found there was, within me, an invincible summer.
And that makes me happy. For it says that no matter how hard the world pushes against me, within me, there's something stronger – something better, pushing right back.

Truly yours, Albert Camus

℘

If I Should Never See The Moon Again
Major Malcolm Boyle

If I should never see the moon again
Rising red gold across the harvest field
Or feel the stinging soft rain
As the brown earth her treasures yield.
If I should never taste the salt sea spray
As the ship beats her course across the breeze.
Or smell the dog-rose and new-mown hay,
or moss or primroses beneath the tree.
If I should never hear the thrushes wake
Long before the sunrise in the glimmering dawn.
Or watch the huge Atlantic rollers break
Against the rugged cliffs in baffling scorn.
If I have to say good bye to stream and wood,
To wide ocean and the green clad hill,
I know that he, who made this world so good
Has somewhere made a heaven better still.
This bears witness with my latest breath
Knowing the love of God, I fear no death.

Farm Work Doesn't Make you Stronger

Farm work doesn't make you stronger. It doesn't make you anything. It reveals you.

There's gym strong and then there's farm strong. They're mutually exclusive.

The toughest women you'll ever meet spend their days on a farm.

There are more uses for twixe than you can possibly imagine. You can tie up a hole in a slow feeder, fashion a tail strap for a horse's blanket, mend a broken fence and use it as a belt.

"Well that certainly didn't go as planned," is one thing you'll say quite a bit.

Control is a mere illusion. The thought that you have any, at any given time, is utterly false.

Sometimes sleep is a luxury. So are lunch and dinner. And brushing your hair.

If you've never felt your obliques contract, then you've never tried stopping an overly full wheelbarrow of horse manure from tipping over sideways. Trust me, you'll find muscles that you never knew existed on the human skeleton to prevent this from happening.

When one of the animals is ill, you'll go to heroic lengths to minimise their discomfort.

Their needs come first. In summer heat and coldest winter days. Clean water, clean bed, and plenty of feed. Before you have your first meal, they all eat.

When you lose one of them, even though you know that day is inevitable, you still feel sadness, angst and emotional pain from the top of your head to the tips of your toes. And it's a heaviness that lingers even though you must regroup and press on.

You'll cry a lot. But you'll never live more fully. You'll remain present no matter what because you must. There is no other option.

You'll ask for so many miracles and hold out hope until the very last.

You will, at least once, face-plant in the manure pile.

You'll find yourself saying things like, "we have maybe twenty minutes of daylight left to git 'er done" whilst gazing up at a nonspecific place in the sky.

You'll become weirdly obsessive about the weather.

You'll go out in public wearing filthy clothes and smelling of dirt, sweat and poop. People will look at you sideways and crinkle their noses but you won't care.

Your entire day can derail within ten seconds of the rising sun.

You can wash your coveralls. They won't look any cleaner, but they will smell much nicer.

Farm work is difficult in its simplicity.

You'll always notice just how beautiful sunrises and sunsets really are.

Should you ever have the opportunity to work on a farm, take the chance! You will never do anything more satisfying in your entire life.

cʒ

Until the Wheels Fall Off
Michael Maller

Until the Wheels Fall Off
Patch my holes with duct tape and
Stitch my tears with twine;
Oil my hinges when I creak,
Rotate my tyres when I'm weak.
Just keep me in the game.
I fear no sneeze, no ache, no cough;
I'm on this ride until it stops,
Or until the wheels fall off.
Knit my bones up if they break and
Cast me when I sprain.
Rewind me when my springs are sprung –
Fix me up! I'm far from done –
I will hobble all the way.
Let meeker souls look on and scoff,
I'm on this ride until it stops,
Or all the wheels fall off.

The Robin

The Fine Line of Saving Lives
Duncan Tripp

As a UK Search and Rescue Winchman Paramedic I consider myself to be in a unique and privileged position. There are not many jobs where, in some circumstances, dynamic life and death decision may have to be made in challenging and austere conditions. These decisions may not be isolated to the patient or the victim but be a consideration that I will need to make about my own commitment.

In some circumstances where the options are limited, the use of a SAR helicopter may be the only option and the Winchman becomes the focus. Like a pyramid, with the Winchman at the point, there needs to be a strong foundation. Within the helicopter there is a four-man crew where we rely on each other, respecting one another's capabilities and contribution. This team is arguably the epitome of Crew Resource Management and Human Factors. There is a captain, but it is the whole crew who make decisions as a collective. If anyone is not content with a plan, then they will voice their opinion and a new plan will be conceived. The team train hard together, pushing each other to their limits developing a high degree of empathy, understanding and appreciation of each other's role. This helps to develops a high degree of mutual respect and most decisions come naturally and in harmony. This is one of the key elements in my decision-making process allowing me to develop and define ultimate trust. There are not many jobs where an individual puts his life in the hands of his colleagues – my life in their hands.

We work on a priority of helicopter, Winchman and casualty in that order. There are times when a crew will re-prioritise this in specific situations taking into consideration the risk benefit analysis. Like any organisation there are rules and regulations that we must abide by. However, we are in a very unusual situation where we can treat the rules and regulations as guidelines in order to save life, but each of us must be in agreement and be able to justify our actions. There is a very fine line between saving life, compounding the situation or possibly losing the crew and the helicopter as well as the casualty. This is the balance of judgement that we may need to make, there is no right answer – damned if we do, damned if we don't.

It is not just about us, the pyramid also needs engineers, admin, emergency services, control, tasking communication, friends, family... the list goes on, it becomes a multi-agency, multi-faceted response. Without most of these and the emotional strength and support the pyramid will be weak and unsupportive.

The decision to leave the relatively safe confines of the helicopter can sometimes be at odds with the instinct to live. I know sometimes "it's going to hurt" and don't want to add to the casualty list. In extremes I have felt that I may not return. The consideration is the balance we place on the importance of family and friends. However, the casualty stuck somewhere inaccessible or tossed around in the sea, narrows the options for rescue. That person too has family and friends and without intervention, they may not see them again. My personal considerations and priorities are weighed and the knowledge that if we do not conduct the rescue, then potentially no-one will, the casualty is reliant on us and in some cases the last and only chance they have – we have taken the queens shilling now she expects a return!

A rescue can be physically, mentally and dynamically challenging requiring me to think on my feet. On occasions, once I leave the door, I am on my own with limited communications and at the mercy of the elements, terrain and the crew. In extremist we, and certain Emergency Services or Armed Forces, may knowingly make the decision that will result in the ultimate sacrifice, "that others may live".

Dear One
Max Ehrman

Dear One,
when you are gone,
by day and night
I search,
but find no peace
in anything.
The trees,
the moon,
the sun
no pleasure bring,
As when we two,
star-gazing,
took to flight
To land upon some inner
mountain height.
What joy above the sordid
world to sing
With you who are to me
eternal spring!
I see it now that you
are gone from sight.
But you will come again,
and oh, what joy –
Your cheery voice describing
many a land,
The things men build and
ages long destroy,
We, sitting close together,
hand-in-hand,
Playing as children with
some new-bought toy,
It will be wonderful –
you understand.

Life is amazing.
And then its awful.
And then it's amazing again.
And in between the amazing
and the awful it's ordinary
and mundane and routine.
Breathe in the amazing,
hold on through the awful,
and relax and exhale
during the ordinary.
That's just living,
heartbreaking,
soul healing, amazing,
awful, ordinary life.
And it's breathtakingly
beautiful.

LR Knost

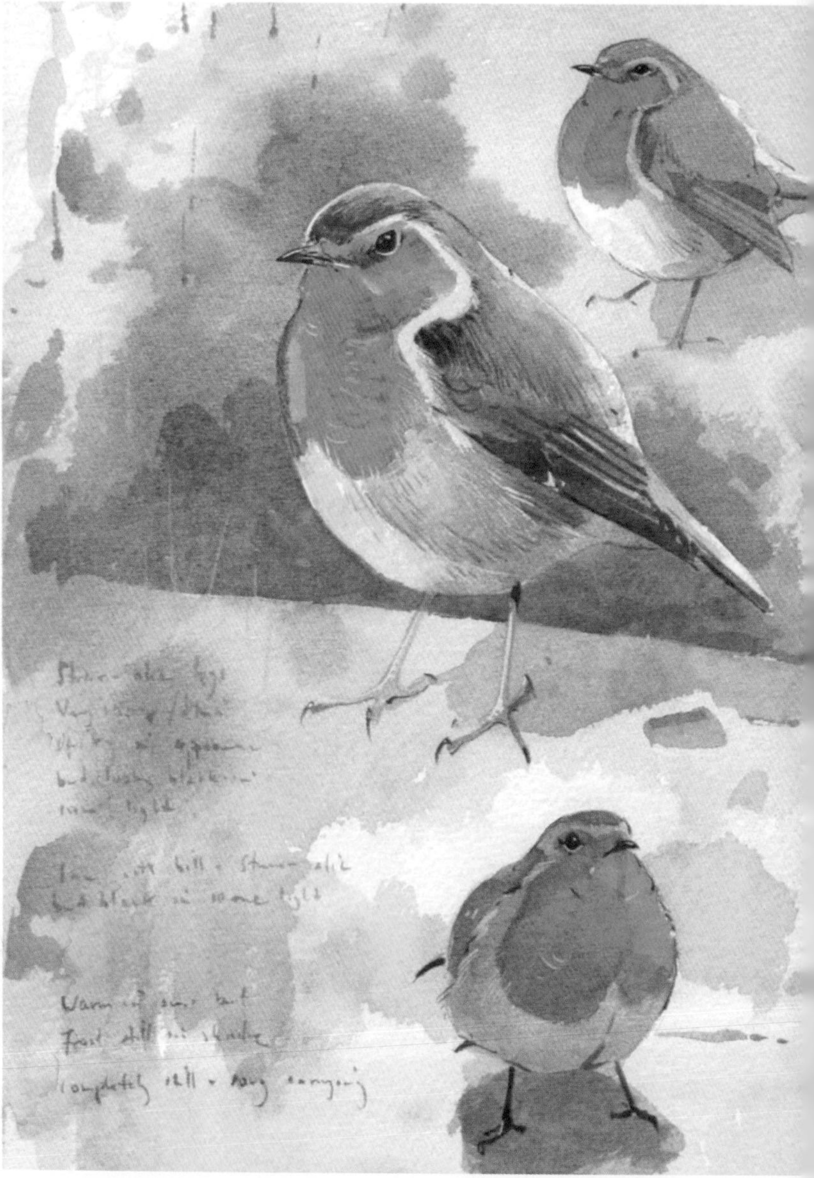

I am the Batman.
Alastair Glennie

It is not who we are underneath but what we do that defines us.
I am the batman. The public sees just another person. Just a GP. Tweed wearing, sensible shoes wearing, sensible car driving, understated and easily overlooked. But under the facade there's a secret. Behind the exterior, behind the mask, is the real person that makes a real difference.

When the bat phone goes off, the sensible car turns into the bat mobile, the shirt and smart trousers are swapped for the bat suit. A tasking to save lives, make a difference and feed a deep urge to help fellow humans in distress. Known only to those who strive for the same ideals, recognised by the few, adding to the team of emergency responders, but paradoxically still very alone in the world. Arriving alone, going home alone. Existing in isolation. And when it's over, back to the cave, few even knowing that the bat was there, those helped assuming it was just all part of the job. The bat staying away from the lime-light, preferring the shadows and anonymity.

Why? Maybe it's healing childhood trauma of a need to make the world happier? Maybe it's to compensate for a career that lacks immediacy? Maybe it's the excitement that comes with cheating death, the adrenaline rush addiction that cannot be found in other ways? Maybe it's for the look on the individuals eyes who has called for help when the help arrive – the bat is here to help. For the calm that follows the hysteria before. The ability to make order out of chaos. But the Batman is no hero. He is flawed. He is complex. He is never satisfied. He is as human as the next person. But he believes that one person can make a difference.

Few even know of the bats existence and even fewer know his real identity. Commissioner Gordon in ambulance control controls the bat phone and has an idea. But officially the bat is just a number on airwave. Alfred who looks after him, who suffers the pain with him, who tries to heal the scars and tells him to drive safely and come back alive as he disappears out of the cave. Only Alfred is his wife. And Lucius Fox. The one who provides the bat with his kit. The recognisable blue bag, the equipment and the suit. Without this the bat is nothing. Fox is Claire and The Sandpiper Trust. The real hero that Scotland deserves, not just the one we need.

It is not who we are underneath but what we do that defines us.
I am the batman.

In Order to be Born...

In order to be born, you needed:

2 parents
4 grandparents
8 great-grandparents
16 second great-grandparents
32 third great-grandparents
64 fourth great-grandparents
128 fifth great-grandparents
256 sixth great-grandparents
512 seventh great-grandparents
1,024 eighth great-grandparents
2,048 ninth great-grandparents.

For you to be born today from 12 previous generations, you
needed a total sum of **4,094** ancestors over the last 400 years.
Think for a moment...

How many struggles?
How many battles?
How much ambition and desire?
How much sadness?
How much happiness?
How many love stories?
How many years spent working to make tomorrow better?
How many expressions of hope for the future?

☙

*That was her magic – she could still see the sunset
even on those darkest days*

Atticus Poetry, Love Her Wild

When Great Trees Fall
Maya Angelou

When great trees fall,
rocks on distant hills shudder,
lions hunker down
in tall grasses,
and even elephants
lumber after safety.

When great trees fall
in forests,
small things recoil into silence,
their senses
eroded beyond fear.

When great souls die,
the air around us becomes
light, rare, sterile.
We breathe, briefly.
Our eyes, briefly,
see with
a hurtful clarity.
Our memory, suddenly sharpened,
examines,
gnaws on kind words
unsaid,
promised walks
never taken.

Great souls die and
our reality, bound to
them, takes leave of us.
Our souls,
dependent upon their
nurture,

now shrink, wizened.
Our minds, formed
and informed by their
radiance,
fall away.
We are not so much maddened
as reduced to the unutterable ignorance
of dark, cold caves.

And when great souls die,
after a period peace blooms,
slowly and always
irregularly. Spaces fill
with a kind of
soothing electric vibration.
Our senses, restored, never
to be the same, whisper to us.
They existed. They existed.
We can be. Be and be
better. For they existed.

ᏣᎦ

Trees, like us, live through the cycles of change that come with the changing seasons. Trees are resilient as they learn to bend with the winds, stand strong in the storms, and yet they continue to grow upward. Trees can teach us that our very existence includes change and transformation.

He Is Not Dead
James Whitcomb Riley

I cannot say, and I will not say
That he is dead. He is just away.
With a cheery smile, and a wave of the hand,
He has wandered into an unknown land
And left us dreaming how very fair
It needs must be, since he lingers there.
And you—oh you, who the wildest yearn
For an old-time step, and the glad return,
Think of him faring on, as dear
In the love of There as the love of Here.
Think of him still as the same. I say,
He is not dead – he is just away.

ॐ

She Asks Me to Kill the Spider
by Rudy Francisco

She asks me to kill the spider.
Instead, I get the most
peaceful weapons I can find.

I take a cup and a napkin.
I catch the spider, put it outside
and allow it to walk away.

If I am ever caught in the wrong place
at the wrong time, just being alive
and not bothering anyone,

I hope I am greeted
with the same kind
of mercy.

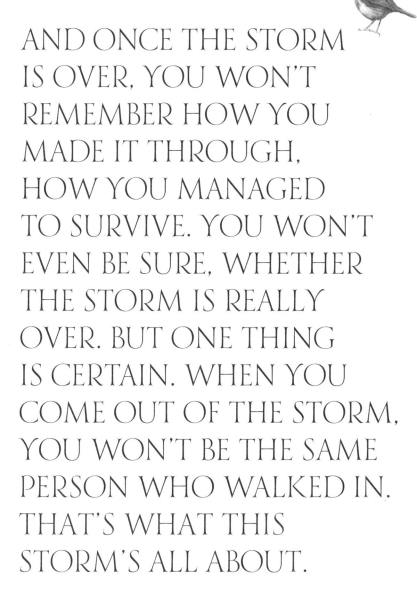

AND ONCE THE STORM
IS OVER, YOU WON'T
REMEMBER HOW YOU
MADE IT THROUGH,
HOW YOU MANAGED
TO SURVIVE. YOU WON'T
EVEN BE SURE, WHETHER
THE STORM IS REALLY
OVER. BUT ONE THING
IS CERTAIN. WHEN YOU
COME OUT OF THE STORM,
YOU WON'T BE THE SAME
PERSON WHO WALKED IN.
THAT'S WHAT THIS
STORM'S ALL ABOUT.

Haruki Murakami

Alright, Here Goes
G Snow

Alright, here goes. I'm old. What that means is that I've survived (so far) and a lot of people I've known and loved did not.

I've lost friends, best friends, acquaintances, co-workers, grandparents, mum, relatives, teachers, mentors, neighbours, and a host of other folks. I have no children, and I can't imagine the pain it must be to lose a child. But here's my two cents.

I wish I could say you get used to people dying. I never did. I don't want to. It tears a hole through me whenever somebody I love dies, no matter the circumstances. But I don't want it to "not matter". I don't want it to be something that just passes.

My scars are a testament to the love and the relationship that I had for and with that person. And if the scar is deep, so was the love. So be it. Scars are a testament to life. Scars are a testament that I can love deeply and live deeply and be cut, or even gouged, and that I can heal and continue to live and continue to love. And the scar tissue is stronger than the original flesh ever was. Scars are a testament to life. Scars are only ugly to people who can't see.

As for grief, you'll find it comes in waves. When the ship is first wrecked, you're drowning, with wreckage all around you. Everything floating around you reminds you of the beauty and the magnificence of the ship that was, and is no more. And all you can do is float. You find some piece of the wreckage and you hang on for a while. Maybe it's some physical thing. Maybe it's a happy memory or a photograph. Maybe it's a person who is also floating. For a while, all you can do is float. Stay alive.

In the beginning, the waves are 100 feet tall and crash over you without mercy. They come 10 seconds apart and don't even give you time to catch your breath. All you can do is hang on and float. After a while, maybe weeks, maybe months, you'll find the waves are still 100 feet tall, but they come further apart. When they come, they still crash all over you and wipe you out. But in between, you can breathe, you can function.

You never know what's going to trigger the grief. It might be a song, a picture, a street intersection, the smell of a cup of coffee. It can be just about anything…and the wave comes crashing. But in between waves, there is life.

Somewhere down the line, and it's different for everybody, you find that the waves are only 80 feet tall. Or 50 feet tall. And while they still come, they come further apart. You can see them coming. An anniversary, a birthday, or Christmas, or landing at O'Hare. You can see it coming, for the most part, and prepare yourself. And when it washes over you, you know that somehow you will, again, come out the other side. Soaking wet, sputtering, still hanging on to some tiny piece of the wreckage, but you'll come out.

Take it from an old guy. The waves never stop coming, and somehow you don't really want them to. But you learn that you'll survive them. And other waves will come. And you'll survive them too. If you're lucky, you'll have lots of scars from lots of loves. And lots of shipwrecks.

Cʐ

Man and Dog
Siegfried Sassoon

Who's this – alone with stone and sky?
It's only my old dog and I – It's only him; it's only me;
Alone with stone and grass and tree.

What share we most – we two together?
Smells, and awareness of the weather.
What is it makes us more than dust?
My trust in him; in me his trust.

Here's anyhow one decent thing
That life to man and dog can bring;
One decent thing, remultiplied
Till earth's last dog and man have died.

The Robin

You Were Here, and Now You are Not
Kathy Galloway, leader of the Iona Community

There is nothing to compare with the pain of death.
You were here, and now you are not. That's all.

I search for you in old photographers, letters,
Things that you touched, Things that remind me of you,
But they cannot fill the space you occupied.
The space is in me too,
Bleeding round the edges where you were torn away.
In the night, strange shapes haunt the space…
Regret, fear, fury,
All the things we might have done.
All the shattered dreams.

How can I go on with this hold inside me?
Partial person!
Don't let me fill the space with the wrong things.
Don't let me cover it up, To eat me from within.
Give me courage to bear my emptiness,
To hold it gently
Till the edges stop bleeding;
Till the darkness becomes friendly;
Till I see the star at its heart;
Till it becomes a fertile space,
Growing new life within it.

If I had not loved, I would not have wept.
This love you have given me;
This love I have carried;
This love has carried me.
And I know that though I cannot see you, touch you,
The love does not go away.
Carried by this love, We are not divided.
And there will be no more weeping.

The Power of the Dog
Rudyard Kipling

There is sorrow enough in the natural way
From men and women to fill our day;
And when we are certain of sorrow in store,
Why do we always arrange for more?
Brothers and Sisters, I bid you beware
Of giving your heart to a dog to tear.

Buy a pup and your money will buy
Love unflinching that cannot lie –
Perfect passion and worship fed
By a kick in the ribs or a pat on the head.
Nevertheless it is hardly fair
To risk your heart for a dog to tear.

When the fourteen years which Nature permits
Are closing in asthma, or tumour, or fits,
And the vet's unspoken prescription runs
To lethal chambers or loaded guns,
Then you will find – it's your own affair –
But… you've given your heart to a dog to tear.

When the body that lived at your single will,
With its whimper of welcome, is stilled (how still!).
When the spirit that answered your every mood
Is gone – wherever it goes – for good,
You will discover how much you care,
And will give your heart to a dog to tear.

We've sorrow enough in the natural way,
When it comes to burying Christian clay.
Our loves are not given, but only lent,
At compound interest of cent per cent.
Though it is not always the case, I believe,
That the longer we've kept 'em, the more do we grieve:
For, when debts are payable, right or wrong,
A short-time loan is as bad as a long – So why in – Heaven
(before we are there) Should we give our hearts to a dog to tear?

If Once You Have Slept On An Island
Rachel Lyman Field

If once you have slept on an island
You'll never be quite the same;
You may look as you looked the day before
And go by the same old name,
You may bustle about in street and shop
You may sit at home and sew,
But you'll see blue water and wheeling gulls
Wherever your feet may go.
You may chat with the neighbours of this and that
And close to your fire keep,
But you'll hear ship whistle and lighthouse bell
And tides beat through your sleep.
Oh! you won't know why and you can't say how
Such a change upon you came,
But once you have slept on an island,
You'll never be quite the same.

cʒ

The Peace of Wild Things
Wendell Berry

When despair for the world grows in me
and I wake in the night at the least sound
in fear of what my life and my children's lives may be,
I go and lie down where the wood drake
rests in his beauty on the water, and the great heron feeds.
I come into the peace of wild things
who do not tax their lives with forethought
of grief. I come into the presence of still water.
And I feel above me the day-blind stars
waiting with their light. For a time
I rest in the grace of the world, and am free.

HEALTH IS THE GREATEST
OF GOD'S GIFTS, BUT WE TAKE IT
FOR GRANTED; YET IT HANGS ON
A THREAD AS FINE AS A SPIDER'S
WEB AND THE TINIEST THING
CAN MAKE IT SNAP, LEAVING
THE STRONGEST OF US HELPLESS
IN AN INSTANT.   *Jennifer Worth*

CB

The Scot Within Me
S Mortazav

Why is it that my heart stirs
When I hear the bagpipes play?
Why do I feel Scotland is my home
When I live so far away?

> Why do I feel a sense of pride
> When I see the Saltire fly?
> Although it may seem strange to you
> Perhaps I can tell you why.

When you are born of Scottish blood
Something strange seems to take place
As if a seed is planted within you
Which makes you fiercely proud of your race.

> This Scottish patriotism never dies
> And in your soul it always remains
> Because Scotland is as much a part of you
> As the blood flowing through your veins.

The Robin

When the world is on your shoulders
Laura Ding-Edwards

When the world is on your shoulders
And your heart feels full of lead
And your stomach churns like butter
And the voice inside your head
Is reminding you of everything
You've ever said or done
All your failures and regrets
All the times your fear has won
Take a minute to remember
That you've survived this all before
You've battled and you've conquered
When you thought you had no more
You are stronger than you realise
You are brave and wise and kind
And you know you're so much bigger
Than the doubts that fill your mind
So breathe it in then let it out
Allow the ebb and flow
You can win this war, you always do
You're a warrior you know.

☙

You fall, you rise, you make mistakes, you live, you learn.
You're human, not perfect. You've been hurt, but you're alive.
Think of what a precious privilege it is to be alive
– to breathe, to think, to enjoy, and to chase the things you love.
Sometimes there is sadness in our journey,
but there is also lots of beauty.
We must keep putting one foot in front of the other
even when we hurt,
for we will never know what is waiting
for us just around the bend.

If it should be that I grow frail and weak
And pain should keep me from my sleep,
Then will you do what must be done,
For this – the last battle – can't be won.
You will be sad I understand,
But don't let grief then stay your hand,
For on this day, more than the rest,
Your love and friendship must stand the test.
We have had so many happy years,
You wouldn't want me to suffer so.
When the time comes, please, let me go.
Take me to where to my needs they'll tend.
Only, stay with me till the end
And hold me firm and speak to me
Until my eyes no longer see.
I know in time you will agree
It is a kindness you do to me.
Although my tail its last has waved,
From pain and suffering I have been saved.
Don't grieve that it must be you
Who has to decide this thing to do;
We've been so close – we two – these years,
Don't let your heart hold any tears.

Anon

Look After You
Anon

I know that it's hard and you feel this pain
But I guess in the end that we all feel the same
In your darkest times I can be the light
I will stand with you now and help you shield the fight
Times are tough and harder times are to come
But know that I'm here even when you feel numb
You might think you've reached the darkest that you can possibly be;
But it's not until then that you will finally see
You're self-worth is more than you'll ever know
It seem like forever, time does go slow
But go easy on yourself: you've got to be kind
Trust in yourself and true love you will find

☙

THOSE WHO ARE NEAR ME DO NOT
KNOW THAT YOU ARE NEARER TO ME
THAN THEY ARE.
THOSE WHO SPEAK TO ME DO NOT
KNOW THAT MY HEART IS FULL WITH
YOUR UNSPOKEN WORDS.
THOSE WHO CROWD IN MY PATH
DO NOT KNOW THAT I AM WALKING
ALONE WITH YOU.
THOSE WHO LOVE ME DO NOT
KNOW THAT THEIR LOVE BRINGS
YOU TO MY HEART.

Tagore

Legacy of Laughter

Anon

Life handed him a few hard knocks;
Sometimes his luck was bad.
He had the usual ups and downs
As most of us have had.

> **Grief had its day along his way,**
> **Great fortune passed him by,**
> **But he always came out a winner**
> **With a twinkle in his eye.**

This legacy of laughter,
A gift from some forbear,
Was all the weapon that he had
To fight life's pain and care.

> **But he kept his sense of humor,**
> **And he laughed away the tears,**
> **And he went on spreading chuckles**
> **All around him down the years.**

And I know I'll find him waiting,
When I join him by and by,
Likely joshing with the angels,
With that twinkle in his eye.

CB

And I raise my eyes to the mountains,
From whence my help shall come.

Psalm 121

The Robin

Me: Hey God.

God: Hello...

Me: I'm falling apart. Can you put me back together?

God: I would rather not.

Me: Why?

God: Because you aren't a puzzle.

Me: What about all of the pieces of my life that are falling down onto the ground?

God: Let them stay there for a while. They fell off for a reason. Take some time and decide if you need any of those pieces back.

Me: You don't understand! I'm breaking down!

God: No – you don't understand. You are breaking through. What you are feeling are just growing pains. You are shedding the things and the people in your life that are holding you back. You aren't falling apart. You are falling into place. Relax. Take some deep breaths and allow those things you don't need any more to fall off of you. Quit holding onto the pieces that don't fit you anymore. Let them fall off. Let them go.

Me: Once I start doing that, what will be left of me?

God: Only the very best pieces of you.

Me: I'm scared of changing.

God: I keep telling you – YOU AREN'T CHANGING!!
YOU ARE BECOMING!

Me: Becoming who?

God: Becoming who I created you to be! A person of light and love and charity and hope and courage and joy and mercy and grace and compassion. I made you for more than the shallow pieces you have decided to adorn yourself with that you cling to with such greed and fear. Let those things fall off of you. I love you! Don't change! ... Become! Become! Become who I made you to be. I'm going to keep telling you this until you remember it.

Me: There goes another piece.

God: Yep. Let it be.

Me: So ... I'm not broken?

God: Of course Not! – but you are breaking like the dawn.
It's a new day. Become!!!

Anon

284

What moves through us
is a silence, a quiet sadness,
a longing for one more day,
one more word,
one more touch.
We may not understand
why you left this earth
so soon, or why you left
before we were ready to
say goodbye,
but little-by-little,
we begin to remember
not just that you died,
but that you lived.
And that your life gave
us memories
too beautiful to forget.

BJ Karrer

My Get Up and Go Has Got Up and Went
John Denham

My get up and go has got up and went
How do I know that my youth is all spent?
Well, my get up and go has got up and went.

But in spite of it all I am able to grin
when I recall where my get up has been.
Old age is golden – so I've heard it said –
but sometimes I wonder when I get into bed,
with my ears in a drawer and my teeth in a cup,
my eyes on the table until I wake up.

Ere sleep dims my eyes I say to myself,
"Is there anything else I should lay on the shelf?"
And I'm happy to say as I close my door,
my friends are the same, perhaps even more.

When I was young, my slippers were red,
I could pick up my heels right over my head.
When I grew older, my slippers were blue,
but still I could dance the whole night through.
But now I am old, my slippers are black,
I walk to the store and puff my way back.

The reason I know my youth is all spent,
my get up and go has got up and went.
But I really don't mind when I think, with a grin,
of all the grand places my get up has been.
Since I have retired from life's competition,
I accommodate myself with complete repetition.
I get up each morning, and dust off my wits,
pick up my paper and read the "obits".
If my name is missing, I know I'm not dead,
so I eat a good breakfast and go back to bed

You Think You can Define Me
Erin Hanson

You think you can define me,
That I'm a tick in just one box,
Like my being is a door,
That a single key unlocks,
But let me tell you something,
I have the universe inside,
I have an untold ocean
With a constant changing tide,
I'm home to endless mountains,
With tips that touch the sky,
Flocks of grand migrating birds,
And deserts harsh and dry,
I house the wildest rivers,
And a host of sweeping plains,
I feel in waves of sunshine,
Or in unrelenting rains,
Don't tell me that you know me,
That "this right here is what you are",
I am the universe in motion,
For I was born from the stars.

೫

Every day is a fresh beginning.
Listen my soul to the glad refrain and spite of old sorrows
and older sinnings, troubles forecasted and possible pain,
take heart with the day and begin again.

Susan Coolidge

Rain does not fall on one roof alone

℃₃

The Summer Day
Mary Oliver

Who made the world?
Who made the swan, and the black bear?
Who made the grasshopper?
This grasshopper, I mean –
the one who has flung herself out of the grass,
the one who is eating sugar out of my hand,
who is moving her jaws back and forth instead of up and down –
who is gazing around with her enormous and complicated eyes.
Now she lifts her pale forearms and thoroughly washes her face.
Now she snaps her wings open, and floats away.
I don't know exactly what a prayer is.
I do know how to pay attention, how to fall down
into the grass, how to kneel down in the grass,
how to be idle and blessed, how to stroll through the fields,
which is what I have been doing all day.
Tell me, what else should I have done?
Doesn't everything die at last, and too soon?
Tell me, what is it you plan to do
with your one wild and precious life?

LOVE,
AS POWERFUL AS
YOUR MOTHER'S
FOR YOU
LEAVES ITS OWN
MARK.
NOT A SCAR,
NO VISIBLE SIGN.
TO HAVE BEEN LOVED
SO DEEPLY EVEN
THOUGH THE PERSON
WHO LOVED US IS
GONE, WILL GIVE US
SOME PROTECTION
FOR EVER.
IT IS IN YOUR VERY
SKIN.

Albus Dumbledore

Not Growing Old
John E. Roberts

They say that I am growing old;
I've heard them tell it times untold,
In language plain and bold –
But I am NOT growing old.

This frail old shell in which I dwell
Is growing old, I know full well –
But I am not the shell.

What if my hair is turning grey?
Grey hairs are honorable, they say.
What if my eyesight's growing dim?
I still can see to follow him
Who sacrificed His life for me
Upon the cross of Calvary.

What should I care if Time's old plow
Has left its furrows on my brow?
Another house, not made with hand,
Awaits me in the Glory Land.

What though I falter in my walk?
What though my tongue refuse to talk?
I still can tread the narrow way,
I still can watch, and praise and pray,

My hearing may not be as keen
As in the past it may have been,
Still, I can hear my Saviour say,
In whispers soft, "This is the way."

The outward man, do what I can
To lengthen out this life's short span,

Shall perish, and return to dust,
As everything in nature must.

The inward man, the Scriptures say,
Is growing stronger every day.
Then how can I be growing old
When safe within my Saviour's fold?

Ere long my soul shall fly away
And leave this tenement of clay;
This robe of flesh I'll drop, and rise
To seize the "everlasting prize."
I'll meet you on the streets of gold,
And prove that I'm not growing old.

☙

IT'S ONE THING
TO FEEL THAT YOU ARE
ON THE RIGHT PATH,
BUT IT'S ANOTHER
TO THINK THAT YOURS
IS THE ONLY PATH

Paulo Coelho, The Alchemist

At Some Point in our Lives We All Age

At some point in our lives we all age; as we get older our skin wrinkles, creases and lines appear. When we are young our skin is springy but as we age our skin loses its flexibility.

Wrinkles are not just a sign of old age but also appear when our skin has been exposed to too much ultra violet light, through sunbathing or spending too much time outdoors.

They say that your skin tells a story.

Your skin is trying to tell you something. It's telling a story about your health, habits and history.

My face is like a character map that defines my life. Fine lines on my forehead, represent my life: My story.

Up until 2 years ago I always thought that my skin was ageing quite well. That was until I received the biggest blow that I had the big C. Since my treatment I seem to have aged ten-fold. Lines appeared along my forehead, creases around my mouth and my hands have aged.

My youthful skin gone; instead replaced with worn out, saggy skin.

I used to fear getting old, now I embrace it. As the proverb says "Grey hair is a crown of glory; it is gained in a righteous life". Grey hair and wrinkles are a sign of a life that has been lived.

These lines across my face tell a story of where I have been and what I have gone through. Just like a scar they are a reminder that life still exists.

Wrinkles around my eyes indicate where laughter and smiles once were. Memories of watching my children, laughing at their antics.

The puffy dry, sunken eyes from all of the tears that have fallen on to the cheeks below.

They show the sheer exhaustion that comes with parenting, the years of sleepless nights and early mornings.

The deep lines show the fear of receiving another diagnosis.

Creases of joy of having a wonderful family and friendship.

Memories of my youth.

They show the loneliness of what Cancer can do to you.

And they show jubilation of bringing up three amazing boys.

But most of all, each and every wrinkle, crease, crow foot and age spot shows thankfulness. Thankful that I live another day, week, month and year to carry on mapping my life.

Every Wrinkle. Every crease. Every flaw. Every age spot. Every detail maps the life that I have lived. A journey that has brought tears, worry, laughter, memories, happiness and sadness.

A journey of life. A journey that, I hope, I will continue on. Adding on more wrinkles and lines in years to come. Adding on to my story. These lines on my face are not wrinkles, they are survival lines. Each telling its own story of happiness and sadness.

❡

Butterfly Kisses
John F Connor

Don't cry for me please don't be sad
Hold on to the memories of the times we both had
Don't dwell on dark thoughts hold on tight to your wishes
Sending you hugs and butterfly kisses
I walk beside you I am there all day long
I am right here but you think I am gone
You don't see me but I can see you
Whatever the problems I will help get you through
I am the wind in your hair and sand in your toes
Butterfly kisses that you feel on your nose
I am with you at sunrise and in sunset
But you can't see me is my one regret
I sit right beside you when you are sad
As you look through the photos of times we both had
I watch you sleeping I hold you so tight
Before I go I kiss you goodnight
I will watch over you from heaven above
Forever you will be my one true love
Hold on to your dreams and all your wishes
Sending you hugs and butterfly kisses

Love is...

First of all, it's a big responsibility, especially in a city like New York.
So think long and hard before deciding on love.
On the other hand, love gives you a sense of security:
when you're walking down the street late at night and you have a leash on love ain't no one going to mess with you.
Because crooks and muggers think love is unpredictable.
Who knows what love could do in its own defence?

On cold winter nights, love is warm.
It lies between you and lives and breathes and makes funny noises.
Love wakes you up all hours of the night with its needs.
It needs to be fed so it will grow and stay healthy.

Love doesn't like being left alone for long.
But come home and love is always happy to see you.
It may break a few things accidentally in its passion for life, but you can never be mad at love for long.

Is love good all the time? No! No!
Love can be bad. Bad, love, bad! Very bad love.

Love makes messes. Love leaves you little surprises here and there.
Love needs lots of cleaning up after.
Sometimes you just want to get love fixed.
Sometimes you want to roll up a piece of newspaper and swat love on the nose, not so much to cause pain, just to let love know Don't you ever do that again!

Sometimes love just wants to go out for a nice long walk.
Because love loves exercise. It will run you around the block and leave you panting, breathless. Pull you in different directions at once, or wind itself around and around you until you're all wound up and you cannot move.

But love makes you meet people wherever you go.

People who have nothing in common but love stop and talk to each other on the street.

Throw things away and love will bring them back, again, and again, and again.
But most of all, love needs love, lots of it.
And in return, love loves you and never stops.

☙

It's Dark Because You are Trying Too Hard
Aldous Huxley

It's dark because you are trying too hard.
Lightly child, lightly. Learn to do everything lightly.
Yes, feel lightly even though you're feeling deeply.
Just lightly let things happen and lightly cope with them.

I was so preposterously serious in those days, such a humorless little prig.
Lightly, lightly – it's the best advice ever given me.
When it comes to dying even.
Nothing ponderous, or portentous, or emphatic.
No rhetoric, no tremolos,
no self-conscious persona putting on its celebrated imitation
of Christ or Little Nell.
And of course, no theology, no metaphysics.
Just the fact of dying and the fact of the clear light.

So throw away your baggage and go forward.
There are quick sands all about you, sucking at your feet,
trying to suck you down into fear and self-pity and despair.
That's why you must walk so lightly.
Lightly my darling,
on tiptoes and no luggage,
not even a sponge bag,
completely unencumbered.

When I Wander
Norman McNamara

When I wander
don't tell me to come and sit down.
Wander with me.
It may be because I am hungry, thirsty, need the toilet.
Or maybe I just need to stretch my legs.

> **When I call for my mother**
> **(even though I'm ninety)**
> **don't tell me she has died.**
> **Reassure me, cuddle me, ask me about her.**
> **It may be that I am looking for the security**
> **that my mother once gave me.**

When I shout out
please don't ask me to be quiet... or walk by.
I am trying to tell you something,
but have difficulty in telling you what.
Be patient. Try to find out.
I may be in pain.

> **When I become agitated or appear angry,**
> **please don't reach for the drugs first.**
> **I am trying to tell you something.**
> **It may be too hot, too bright, too noisy.**
> **Or maybe it's because I miss my loved ones.**
> **Try to find out first.**

When I don't eat my dinner or drink my tea
it may be because I've forgotten how to.
Show me what to do, remind me.
It may be that I just need to hold my knife and fork
I may know what to do then.

When I push you away
while you're trying to help me wash or get dressed,
maybe it's because I have forgotten what you have said.
Keep telling me what you are doing
over and over and over.
Maybe others will think
you're the one that needs the help!

> With all my thoughts and maybes,
> perhaps it will be you
> who reaches my thoughts,
> understands my fears,
> and will make me feel safe.
> Maybe it will be you
> who I need to thank.
> If only I knew how.

 C3

All Suddenly the Wind Comes Soft
Rupert Brooke

All suddenly the wind comes soft
And Spring is here again;
And the hawthorn quickens with buds of green,
And my heart with buds of pain.
My heart all Winter lay so numb,
The earth so dead and frore,
That I never thought the Spring would come,
Or my heart wake any more.
But Winter's broken and earth has woken,
And the small birds cry again;
And the hawthorn hedge puts forth its buds
And my heart puts forth its pain.

The Robin

I've Been very Poorly But Now I Feel Prime

Bob Weston and Bert Lee

I've been very poorly but now I feel prime,
I've been out today for the very first time.
I felt like a lad as I walked down the road,
Then I met Old Jones and he said, 'Well I'm blowed!'
My word, you do look queer!
My word, you do look queer!

Oh, dear! You look dreadful: you've had a near shave,
You look like a man with one foot in the grave.'
I said, 'Bosh! I'm better; it's true I've been ill.'
He said, 'I'm delighted you're better, but still,
I wish you'd a thousand for me in your will.
My word, you do look queer!'

That didn't improve me, it quite put me back,
Still, I walked farther on, and I met Cousin Jack.
He looked at me hard and he murmured, 'Gee whiz!
It's like him! It can't be! It isn't! It is!
By gosh! Who'd have thought it? Well, well, I declare!
I'd never have known you except for your hair.
My word, you do look queer!
My word, you do look queer!

Your cheeks are all sunk and your colour's all gone,
Your neck's very scraggy, still you're getting on.
How old are you now? About fifty, that's true.
Your father died that age, your mother did too.
Well, the black clothes I wore then'll come in for you.
My word! You do look queer!'

That really upset me; I felt quite cast down,
But I tried to buck up, and then up came old Brown.
He stared at me hard, then he solemnly said,
'You shouldn't be out, you should be home in bed.
I heard you were bad, well I heard you were gone.

You look like a corpse with an overcoat on.
My word you do look queer!
My word you do look queer!

You'd best have a brandy before you drop dead.'
So, pale as a sheet, I crawled in the 'King's Head',
The barmaid sobbed, 'Oh you poor fellow,' and then
She said, 'On the slate you owe just one pound ten,
You'd better pay up, we shan't see you again.
My word you do look queer!'

My knees started knocking, I did feel so sad.
Then Brown said, 'Don't die in a pub, it looks bad,'
He said, 'Come with me, I'll show you what to do.
Now I've got a friend who'll be useful to you.'
He led me to Black's Undertaking Depot,
And Black, with some crepe round his hat said, 'Hello,
'My word you do look queer!
My word you do look queer!

Now we'll fix you up for a trifling amount.
Now what do you say to a bit on account?'
I said, 'I'm not dying.' He said, 'Don't say that!
My business of late has been terribly flat,
But I'm telling my wife she can have that new hat!
My word, you do look queer!'

I crawled in the street and I murmured, 'I'm done.'
Then up came Old Jenkins and shouted, 'By gum!'
'My word you do look well!
My word you do look well!
You're looking fine and in the pink!'
I shouted, 'Am I?... Come and have a drink!
You've put new life in me, I'm sounder than a bell.
By gad! There's life in the old dog yet.
My word, I do feel well!'

When I'm an Old Lady
and Live With My Kids
May Baker Winke

When I'm an old lady, I'll live with each kid, and
bring so much happiness, just as they did.
I want to pay back all the joy they've provided.
Returning each deed! Oh, they'll be so excited!
(When I'm an old lady and live with my kids.)
I'll write on the wall with reds, whites and blues,
and I'll bounce on the furniture wearing my shoes.
I'll drink from the carton and then leave it out.
I'll stuff all the toilets and oh, how they'll shout!
(When I'm an old lady and live with my kids.)
When they're on the phone and just out of reach,
I'll get into things like sugar and bleach.
Oh, they'll snap their fingers and then shake
their head, and when that is done, I'll hide under
the bed!
(When I'm an old lady and live with my kids.)
When they cook dinner and call me to eat,
I'll not eat my green beans or salad or meat,
I'll gag on my okra, spill milk on the table,
and when they get angry, I'll run... if I'm able!
(When I'm an old lady and live with my kids.)
I'll sit close to the TV, I'll click through the
channels, I'll cross both eyes just to see if they
stick. I'll take off my socks and throw one away,
and play in the mud till the end of the day!
(When I'm an old lady and live with my kids.)
And later in bed, I'll lay back and sigh,
I'll thank God in prayer and then close my eyes.
My kids will look down with a smile slowly
creeping, and say with a groan,
"She's so sweet when she's sleeping!"

I Sit Beside the fire and think
J R R Tolkein

I sit beside the fire and think
of all that I have seen
of meadow-flowers and butterflies
in summers that have been;

> Of yellow leaves and gossamer
> in autumns that there were,
> with morning mist and silver sun
> and wind upon my hair.

I sit beside the fire and think
of how the world will be
when winter comes without a spring
that I shall ever see.

> For still there are so many things
> that I have never seen:
> in every wood in every spring
> there is a different green.

I sit beside the fire and think
of people long ago
and people who will see a world
that I shall never know.

> But all the while I sit and think
> of times there were before,
> I listen for returning feet
> and voices at the door.

The Carrot, the Egg, and the Coffee Beans

A young woman went to her mother and told her about her life and how things were so hard for her. She did not know how she was going to make it and wanted to give up. She was tired of fighting and struggling.

It seemed that, as one problem was solved, a new one arose. Her mother took her to the kitchen. She filled three pots with water and placed each on a high fire. Soon the pots came to a boil. In the first, she placed carrots, in the second she placed eggs, and in the last she placed ground coffee beans.

She let them sit and boil, without saying a word. In about twenty minutes, she turned off the burners. She fished the carrots out and placed them in a bowl. She pulled the eggs out and placed them in a bowl. Then she ladled the coffee out and placed it in a bowl. Turning to her daughter, she asked, "Tell me, what do you see?"

"Carrots, eggs, and coffee," the young woman replied. The mother brought her closer and asked her to feel the carrots. She did and noted that they were soft. She then asked her to take an egg and break it. After pulling off the shell, she observed the hard-boiled egg. Finally, she asked her to sip the coffee. The daughter smiled as she tasted its rich aroma. The daughter then asked, "What does it mean, mother?"

Her mother explained that each of these objects had faced the same adversity – boiling water – but each reacted differently.

THE CARROT

The carrot went in strong, hard and unrelenting. However, after being subjected to the boiling water, it softened and became weak.

THE EGG

The egg had been fragile. Its thin outer shell had protected its liquid interior. But, after sitting through the boiling water, its inside became hardened!

THE COFFEE BEANS

The coffee beans were unique, however. After they were in the boiling water, they had changed the water.

"Which are you?" the mother asked her daughter. "When adversity knocks on your door, how do you respond? Are you a carrot, an egg, or a coffee bean?" Think of this: Which am I? Am I the carrot that seems strong but, with pain and adversity, do I wilt and become soft and lose my strength? Am I the egg that starts with a malleable heart, but changes with the heat? Did I have a fluid spirit but, after a death, a breakup, or a financial hardship, does my shell look the same, but on the inside am I bitter and tough with a stiff spirit and a hardened heart? Or am I like the coffee bean? The bean actually changes the hot water, the very circumstance that brings the pain. When the water gets hot, it releases the fragrance and flavour.

If you are like the bean, when things are at their worst, you get better and change the situation around you. When the hours are the darkest and trials are their greatest, do you elevate to another level? How do you handle adversity? Are you a carrot, an egg, or a coffee bean?

☙

The greater your storm…
the brighter your rainbow

When I Moved to Scotland...
Dr Tom Mallinson

When I moved to Scotland and was fortunate enough to be issued with a big blue 'Sandpiper Bag' filled with emergency medical equipment. I had never heard of The Sandpiper Trust and I certainly knew very little about sandpipers or the connection to pre-hospital care.

I did some research into The Sandpiper Trust and discovered how a tragic event led to the long lasting legacy in relation to prehospital care. I mostly stopped pondering the sandpiper, and concentrated more on the logo on my Sandpiper bag and its contents as well as my exceptionally warm and visible jacket which keeps me safe whilst responding to urgent calls.

Two days ago, I was walking my dog along the beach, and spotted a little bird – blending in with its surroundings, unobtrusive – rushing into the turbulent surf, darting into the chaos and re-emerging and once again disappearing amongst the pebbles on the beach. I was struck by the similarities between the sandpiper bird and myself, a sandpiper responder.

Our day jobs, no-one knowing about the big blue bag in the boot of our cars – we go unseen, just like the sandpiper on the beach. Then day or night, we might be asked to drop what we are doing and rush into the chaos – much like the diminutive sandpiper bird, hopefully providing the urgent care, assistance, and treatment to a victim of an accident or medical emergency in their time of need.

Afterwards, we slip away, back to our daily lives, unobserved and un-noticed. The Sandpiper Bag is yet again tucked into the boot of our cars, along with the high-visibility jacket.

Like our avian namesake, Sandpiper responders are ubiquitous across Scotland, rushing into chaos, and then slipping away. I am proud to be in possession of one of the easy recognisable blue Sandpiper Bags. Sandpiper has done an amazing job of providing these life-saving kit bags throughout Scotland.

Woodland Burial
Pam Ayres

Don't lay me in some gloomy churchyard shaded by a wall
Where the dust of ancient bones has spread a dryness over all,
Lay me in some leafy loam where, sheltered from the cold
Little seeds investigate and tender leaves unfold.
There kindly and affectionately, plant a native tree
To grow resplendent before God and hold some part of me.
The roots will not disturb me as they wend their peaceful way
To build the fine and bountiful, from closure and decay.
To seek their small requirements so that when their work is done
I'll be tall and standing strongly in the beauty of the sun.

ଔ

" You don't 'get over' the man, though you do after a year or two get over the death."
" But you have to learn to live in another country in which you're an unwilling refugee"

Katherine Whitehorn

I'm Fine Thank You *Constance O'Neon*

There is nothing the matter with me
I'm as healthy as can be.
I have arthritis in both my knees
And when I talk, I talk with a wheeze,
My pulse is weak and my blood is thin,
But I'm awfully well for the shape I'm in.
Sleep is denied me night after night,
But every morning I find I'm all right,
My memory is failing, my head's in a spin
But I'm awfully well for the shape I'm in.
The moral is this – as my tale I unfold,
That for you and me who are growing old,
It's better to say, "I'm fine" with a grin,
Than to let folks know the shape we're in.
How do I know that my youth is all spent?
Well my 'get up and go' has got up and went.
But I don't really mind when I think with a grin,
Of all the grand places 'my get up' has been.
Old age is golden, I've heard it said,
But sometimes I wonder as I get into bed,
With my ears in the drawer, my teeth in the cup,
My eyes on the table until I wake up.
Ere sleep overtakes me, I think to myself
Is there anything else I could lay on the shelf?
When I was young, my slippers were red;
I could kick my heels right over my head.
When I got older, my slippers were blue;
But still I could dance the whole night through.
But now I am old, my slippers are black;
I walk to the store and puff my way back.
I get up each day and dust off my wits,
And pick up the paper and read the 'obits'.
If my name is still missing, I know I'm not dead –
So I have a good breakfast and go back to bed.

The Robin

Trauma Permanently Changes Us   *Catherine Woodiwiss*

This is the big, scary truth about trauma: there is no such thing as "getting over it." The five stages of grief model marks universal stages in learning to accept loss, but the reality is in fact much bigger: a major life disruption leaves a new normal in its wake. There is no "back to the old me." You are different now, full stop.

This is not a wholly negative thing. Healing from trauma can also mean finding new strength and joy. The goal of healing is not a papering-over of changes in an effort to preserve or present things as normal. It is to acknowledge and wear your new life- warts, wisdom, and all - with courage.

ა

I hope you are blessed with a heart like a wildflower. Strong enough to rise again after being trampled upon, tough enough to weather the worst of the summer storms, and able to grow and flourish even in the most broken places.

Nikita Gil

ა

You either get bitter or you get better.
It's that simple.
You either take what has been dealt to you and allow it
to make you a better person, or you allow it to tear you down.
The choice does not belong to fate, it belongs to you

Josh Shipp

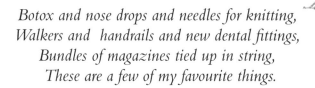

Botox and nose drops and needles for knitting,
Walkers and handrails and new dental fittings,
Bundles of magazines tied up in string,
These are a few of my favourite things.

Cadillacs and cataracts, hearing aids and glasses,
Polident and Fixodent and false teeth in glasses,
Pacemakers, golf carts and porches with swings,
These are a few of my favourite things.

When the pipes leak, When the bones creak,
When the knees go bad,
I simply remember my favorite things,
And then I don't feel so bad.

Hot tea and crumpets and corn pads for bunions,
No spicy hot food or food cooked with onions,
Bathrobes and heating pads and hot meals they bring,
These are a few of my favourite things.

Back pain, confused brains and no need for sinnin',
Thin bones and fractures and hair that is thinnin',
And we won't mention our short shrunken frames,
When we remember our favourite things.

When the joints ache, When the hips break,
When the eyes grow dim,
Then I remember the great life I've had,
And then I don't feel so bad.

For Years the Riverbank was Where *Jill Eisnaugle*

For years, the riverbank was where
Your soul felt most at peace
Your heart was most content when there
With the fish and the geese
But then, your spirit came to rest
Where angels chose to roam
And once equipped with ten pound test
You made yourself at home.

The sky became your deep blue sea
The clouds became your shore
And there, for all eternity
You sat with friends galore
Each angel was a fisherman
Who had traded his pole
For golden wings and a game plan
At Heaven's Fishing Hole.

The tales you told about each catch
Its stature and its girth
Will live in memories unmatched
As days pass here on earth
Until we meet again, one day
Upon God's golden sand
We'll picture you, no other way
Than with a pole in hand.

☙

Faith consists in believing what reason cannot

Voltaire

LISTEN TO THE MUSTN'TS,
CHILD. LISTEN TO THE DON'TS.
LISTEN TO THE SHOULDN'TS,
THE IMPOSSIBLES, THE WON'TS.
LISTEN TO THE NEVER HAVES,
THEN LISTEN CLOSE TO ME...
ANYTHING CAN HAPPEN, CHILD.
ANYTHING CAN BE.

Shel Silverstein

☙

And, one day
I looked back for you
But you weren't there anymore
A stranger did I see
Looking back at me
And, in that very moment
I did promise
That I would keep on looking back for you
As I know
One day
I will
See you again

Athey Thompson

The Robin

The Many Faces of Grief   *A van der Velden*

Robert still cannot sleep too well, he's awake from 2am.
Janet is the opposite, and she doesn't rise till ten.

Sarah made a special card, for each and everyone.
She did this sitting on the beach, while soaking up the sun.

Samuel went out to the shed, in the middle of the night.
He grabbed the axe and chopped the wood, until it was first light.

George took out his little boat, an sailed across the bay.
We may be family, we may be friends, but we each grieve in our own way.

Peter flew off the handle, anything set him off.
Pat put a message in a balloon and gently set it aloft.
Tui simply went to bed and hid under the sheets.
She couldn't bear to leave the house, it's now been several weeks.

Jane cleaned the entire house, from room to room she went.
Till the house was cleaner than it had ever been,
and all her tears were spent.

Leo couldn't wash at all, he didn't shower for days.
We may be friends or family but we grieve in different ways.

Mark just HAD to go to work to " take his mind off things",
Melissa walked to the park at dusk and sat quietly on the swings.
Bethany went down to the gym, she didn't do this for fun,
And if that didn't help to ease her pain, she'd head out for a run.

Patricia looks like nothing's wrong, that not a tear was shed,
Plenty have been but no one knows, she only cries in bed.

So please be kind and patient when loved ones pass away,
For each of us is grieving in our own and special way.

"Who am I?" You ask
I am made from all the people
I've encountered and all the things
I have experienced.
Inside, I hold the laughter
of my friends,
The arguments with my parents,
The chattering of young children,
The warmth of kind strangers.
Inside, there are stitchings
from cracked hearts,
bitter words from
heated arguments,
music that gets me through
and emotions I cannot convey.
I am made from all these people
and moments.
That is who I am.

The Robin

FOR A LITTLE WHILE
I LOOKED OUT AT
THE NIGHT, MY
EYES WANDERING
FROM STAR TO
STAR; AND
I THOUGHT HOW
SMALL ARE ALL
OUR CARES, AND
HOW USELESS OUR
DAILY POTHER!

Max Ehrmann

One Ring, That's All
Aly Dickson

One ring, that's all,
One call that says it all,
One knowing look –
that's all it took
To reach the bounds of human frailty.

You know you know – there is no more to know –
no more that can be done.
One tear, in fear,
now falls – a rivulet of love for
A curly headed boy who smiles –
Our son.

Tell me it's not true.
We knew: no miracle would lead us through
the finality of death –
one gasping breath.
Our frozen hearts dimly veil reality.

We weep, try sleep, but wakefully learn
lives can never be undone.
Our love for one above
now rests by an aura-lit stone for
A curly headed boy who smiles –
Our son.

Take my hand and lead me
Feed my soul – now at last he's free
a falcon still soaring
ponies mad galloping
To live like a child for eternity.
A curly headed boy who smiles – our son.

Poem written by the father of Sandy Dickson
in whose memory Sandpiper was established

Should we lose each
other in the shadow
of the evening trees,
I'll wait for you.
And should I fall
behind, wait for me.

Bruce Springsteen

*Contributed by Claire Maitland in memory of her husband
Robin Maitland (1956-2019) to whom this book is also dedicated.*

*The owl at the top of this page and the illustrations in this section were created by Robin in the year before
he died. He drew them with his left hand and was inspired by Cath, his wonderful occupational therapist.*

Dowalty Skies

Drifting through our childhood
Your lyrics helped us grow
They made us strong and loving
They taught us what we know

Our journeys, short adventures
some far, some wide
Opened doors to all our futures
You're the captain leading our side.

The stars the trees the beasts Burnside
A dram, home's views, forever in you eyes.
The Cairn O'Mount, it's hills in purple bloom,
The towering clouds up there with you
Up night in Dowalty skies.

The courage you wore through the bleakest of storms
Was a lesson to us all
You gave us tools to fight the pain
And to raise creatures loud and small.

The flowers that you created
And the miracle buds to come
Will cheer and laugh and honour your smile
But we will miss you forever numb.

For even though the sun has set upon your Fields of Gold
You planted seeds, mighty and strong
So the memories can never grow old.

by Harry Maitland in memory of his father, Robin Maitland 1956-2019
Harry wrote this the night Robin died.

Robin wrote this story on his iPad with his left hand,
to my sister's grandchildren whilst in hospital
and asked me to share it with you.

You can tell Amy (5), Zoe (3) and Sophie (1) about who came to visit me yesterday. A red squirrel! I saw him come in the door of my room and he ran under my bed and then jumped up onto the windowsill. Seeing that he couldn't get out, he ran around a trolley with my equipment on it and stopped on my pillow next to my face. He asked me what was the best way to get back outside. We discussed it for a while – it was amazing how well we could understand each other – and I suggested that he go back through the door and run down to the end of the corridor where the nurses could open the fire escape door and he can get out. That afternoon, a squirrel waved at me from outside, but it was too far away for me to be sure whether it was in my new friend or not!!

It was an exciting day.

Love Robin x

Acknowledgments

The first edition of *The Swallow, the Owl and the Sandpiper* has found itself on bookshelves, bedside tables, in backpacks and all sorts of places around the world. Continued sales have enabled *Sandpiper* to provide lifesaving equipment to doctors, nurses and paramedics throughout rural Scotland and have saved many lives. I have been spurred on by many to compile a second book; it now includes the resilience of The Little Red Robin. At times I have found it challenging without the guidance of my husband, Robin, who supported me through the first book. I cannot give enough praise to all who cared for Robin from 2014 to 2019: Scottish Ambulance Service (a special thanks to Keith Jensen); Emergency department; Intensive and HDU care in Aberdeen; both primary and secondary care clinicians; the nursing team at the Glen O' Dee Hospital in Banchory; Lesley of Spear Physio; and his wonderful team of carers who looked after him 24/7 at home and in hospital until he took his last breath.

I would like to acknowledge and thank the following: Firstly, my four children, Harry, Cara, Anna and Jack, who have kept me grounded, even on days when I have felt myself veering dangerously close to the rocks. Penny and Aly Dickson; *Sandpiper* was set up in memory of their son, Sandy. Dr Ewen McLeod, Medical Adviser to *Sandpiper*, has somehow continued to keep us all on the straight and narrow for the past 20 years! Our Patron, Gavin Hastings for his friendship and support both to the charity and to the family throughout Robin's illness.

Thank you to all who took the time to share their favourite words, and to the authors, without whom, this book simply wouldn't exist. A special mention goes to Paul Breen and Lucia Cioffi for sharing their own personal journeys through illness. Their words show us the importance of determination, combined with a touch of humour. The sensitive artwork provided by talented, Fife based artist, Derek Robertson and Fiona Hill, for her skill in designing and putting this book together.

My thanks also to *Sandpiper* fellow trustees, both past and present, for the belief that they have in the work of the charity and also to Lorna Duff, *Sandpiper* manager for all the work she does behind the scenes. Dr Colville Laird, (ex-BASICS-Scotland) without whose foresight and dedication, *Sandpiper* would not exist.

Finally, I would like to pay special tribute to four dedicated supporters of *Sandpiper*, sadly no longer with us: Alexander Aberdeen, Kate Robertson, Miranda McHardy and Dr Mark Bloch.

I have tried to meet copyright requirements and trace authors but in many cases this has proved impossible for which I apologise. All funds raised as a result of sales of this book help to provide emergency pre-hospital care equipment in Scotland.

Claire Maitland MBE

Contributors

Alastair Glennie

Alisdair Aird

Alistair Dickson

Amelia Etherington

Anna Chetland

Anne Moore

Annie Lennox

Anushi Desai

Ava Maitland

Avery House

Barbara Manson

Cara Vincent

Charlotte Kennedy

Christina Robb

Claire Barron

Claire Robertson

David Carroll

Derek Robertson

Donna Ashworth

Duncan Tripp

Eira Nickson

Fabienne Harrison

Fiona Hill

Gavin Hastings

George Berstan

Gordon Riley

Harry Maitland

Heather Morrison

Jac Chetland

Jack Greer

Jack Maitland

James Burnett of Leys

Janey Heaney

Joanna Aberdeen

Kate Nicolson

Katherine Whitehorn

Keith Jenson

Louisa Dickson

Lucy Campbell

Maggie Heath

Mark Beaumont

Maureen Vincent

Milly Forbes-Leith

Miranda McHardy

Molly Arbuthnott

Neil Andrew

Olivia Gillespie

Paul Breen

Penny Dickson

Rae Woodrow

Rev Neil Gardner

Sandy Rough

Saskia Robertson

Sophie MacAulay

Stuart Strachan

Suzanne Drysdale

Tom Mallinson

Wendy Chetland

Wren Hughes

Index of First Lines